Little Black Book for Employment
A Recruiters guide for job seekers

Copyright 2012 by Scott A. Coulte

Published in the United States of America

Little Black Book for Employment
A Recruiters guide for job seekers

ISBN 13: 978-1470092979
ISBN 10: 1470092972

www.scottacoulter.com

Warning-Disclosure:

This Little Black Book for Employment

This book belongs to:

Name: _____

Date: _____

Title: _____

Employment Goals

_____

_____

_____

_____

Table of Contents

Phase One Preparation

Chapter 1 Childlike Ambitions   1
Chapter 2 Unlock your potential for success   5
Chapter 3 Are you employable?   26
Chapter 4 Career Mapping   40
Chapter 5 Time to make the donuts   51
Chapter 6 Goal setting for the professional   60
Chapter 7 Networking   71
Chapter 8 Using technology to find jobs   82
Chapter 9 Developing a winning sales script   86

Phase Two: Execution

Chapter 10 Dialing for dollars   93
Chapter 11 Door to door hunting   104
Chapter 12 Working with recruiters   111
Chapter 13 Interviews   121
Chapter 14 Job search activity   136

Task Summary Page   151

Personal Development Plan   175

Index   178

About the Author   183

Foreword

Over the last 20+ years, I've been blessed to have an impact on the lives of so many people. I realize early in my career that my purpose was to educate and hire those who seek employment. Becoming a professional recruiter was the platform I needed to understand economic workforce dynamics and how people fit in the circle of opportunity.

While recruiting, the industry introduced a multi-generational workforce challenge to me. Economist are focusing on the big three; Baby Boomers, Generation X and the upcoming Generation Y. Each generational workforce has a characteristic that has a profound effect on the business outlook.

I've worked with employers welcoming the Baby Boomers because they are perceived as being hard working, dependent and willing to go the extra mile professionals. Other employers prefer Generation X employees who are considered more aggressive. This is the middle aged crowd who's technically savvy and more open to change in the workplace. I even had clients who preferred a blend of generations. The Baby Boomers would fulfill the leadership roles, and younger generations would be the future replacement staff. On the inside of the company it works perfectly, but to job seekers, it makes looking for career more difficult.

Then comes Generation Y. This extraordinary group of new professionals are fast tracking technology and developing a new world order with home based jobs, virtual support and online solutions. However, their employability brand is a lot different from the other two generations. Generation X and Y are next in line after the Baby Boomers retire.

Three types of job seekers today

Finding employment today is a true challenge for each group. There are three generations of professionals inside the current workforce. Three extremely different approaches to finding employment and career development. For instance, one job opening will have two interviews in the same day. One interview will be with a 27 year old college graduate with spiked hair, straight legged slacks carrying a laptop sporting no necktie. The next interview would be a Baby Boomer wearing a conservative business dress with low heeled shoes and a hard copy resume in hand. Both candidates are qualified, and dressed according to their generational values. Who gets hired?

My motivation to write

My motivation to write this book was driven by a passion to help people. The goal is to help "Old School" and the "New School" job seekers maximize their potential using a blend of generational business tools.

I've heard numerous job coaches guide prospects toward changing who they are following occupational trends issued by the federal government. Trends do not equate to immediate employment. What is trending today may not fit within your expertise. My philosophy is, discover your potential, develop a niche in your industry and life will be full of success.

The same principle applies to employment. I do believe everyone must make certain changes to keep up with today's workforce. This does not mean follow the trends. Be innovative, but don't follow the crowd. For instance, computer classes to become comfortable with social media or break fix would be considered part of professional evolution.

In other cases, to be forced in to a software development course late in your career because your counselor is filling class seats, is not an appropriate career plan if you hate computers. I find mostly Baby Boomers in computer classes who appear to be wasting time and money.

What I find amusing, is Generation Y candidates growing beards because job coaches instruct them to appear older for interviews.

In other words, trying to reinvent yourself outside of your natural characteristics, leads to wasted time and efforts. There is no true future in developing a resume filled with newly learned skills that don't fit your passions.

In over 20 years in personnel, I've had clients who already had an ideal candidate in mind. I've also seen employers give a detailed description of race, gender and experience to recruiters to maximize the talent sourcing process. My philosophy has always been one of opportunity meeting the opportunist. All the job seeker needs is to find the manager who's looking for someone just like them. It's just that simple, right? Not quite that simple but, if you combine the right processes and effort, you can increase your odds significantly. Very similar to what my father told me when I began to date. He said, "There is someone out there for everyone son. You'll look for her and she'll be looking for you. You will know each other when you finally meet"

I've read tons of "How to" books and "1-2-3 Steps" to finding something or another and most of them seem to be focused on a cookie cut process for success. Meaning, everyone has the same skills and same skill weaknesses to be corrected. My approach is based on self assessments and building a direction from there. We aren't baking cakes. Nor are we using the same ingredients every time.

We are building careers for long-term sustainability, and that takes time.

Your perfect search needs the correct blend of other ingredients that may not be listed on the recipe for employment.

Finding out who you are and what you were born to do, is more valuable than trying to follow the hot occupational trends. I want you to focus on companies that hire your expertise. Develop a game plan for companies that are seeking your skill set and make it your job to get in front of the right person. Become an opportunist, one who knows exactly what he or she wants. Establish a plan of action, even if its short-term at first.

Who is this book for?

Its purpose was to provide "every" professional a reference to be innovative using employment tools that lead toward professional growth. What if I'm already employed? This book will help you too. Setting goals, professional assessments, business research, and industry knowledge can be helpful in any area of expertise. Working professionals could develop a career map that could lead to a promotion or better opportunities in the industry. .

Each topic will place the reader in control of his or her own success. Incorporating activities like business research, cold calling and door to door fact finding tactics, readers will begin to develop a blend of core activities that lead toward meeting your workforce goals. Employment trends show that professionals who have no physical activity included in the process eventually leads to no activity over time. They become couch potatoes and have extended periods of unemployment. *The Little Black Book for Employment* will teach you employability branding, and help you face job seeking fears that have kept you stagnate in the past.

Some information on my company

APSI is a consulting and training organization that focus on organizational development, project management, staff augmentation and custom training curriculum.

APSI's clients benefit from having successful executives provide a variety of solutions to increase their workforce productivity. Our consultants are Master Value Wave Practitioners, Six Sigma Certified, Project Managers, Staffing Experts, PHR, Published Authors and accomplished corporate speakers. www.apsicorp.com

APSI's Workforce Development Programs

Through my company APSI, I've spent years helping non-profits and academic institutions identify and develop workforce based courses designed to increase student participation and job placement. My team of OD and training experts offer one or two day workshop to assess and develop your corporate training plans.

During that assessment, we also measure the institutional training expectations in comparison to the workforce demand for skilled workers. APSI's training workshops are interactive and include gap analysis and process improvement tools to position each individual for future growth.

APSI Technical Training Programs

APSI is a licensed Fiber Optic Association (FOA) and Electronic Technician Association (ETA) vocational school. We offer a variety of technical courses ranging from Telecommunications, Fiber Optics, Premise Cabling, Workforce Professional Course, to Customer Services and Sales. Student benefit from having industry experts teach the work ready courses.

Each of our technical programs has over 50% hands on laboratory practice. The FOA and ETA courses are accredited and carry globally recognized credentials.

Custom Training Courses

Partnered with globally recognized Author and organizational development expert Wade Younger, I'm tasked to develop custom training programs for clients to enhance employee skills. These custom programs are designed to help managers assess the internal workforce, and building more effective business group.

While many companies prefer using traditional academic institutions, our clients have found significant returns using our organizational development team to devise a plan based on their specific training needs.

Our flexibility supports the overall priority set by the stakeholders in the company. The result is a custom program with longer term investment returns.

Contact Scott A. Coulter or APSI

My goal is always to leave something behind that will help improve the quality of life from those I come across. Since writing this book, I am developing a newer version to include a one or two day workshop that will allow participants to expand their social skills and expand their professional employability.

If you are interested in having me or one of our corporate speakers consult with your team, contact us at:

APSI
5100 Reagan Drive, Charlotte, NC 28206
www.apsicorp.com or www.scottacoulter.com

Introduction

In early 2008, America began to feel some subtle affects of what would eventually be considered as the greatest recessions since the "Great Depression". In 2011, national unemployment levels nearly reached double digits. I believe this new recession was the byproduct of liberal Federal Reserve policies, reckless banking practices and high levels of bad debt throughout the U.S. Over this 3 to 4 year period, most Chief Executive and Financial Officers began to "cut the fat" or "get lean" to salvage the profits that were left from the downturn.

While many of the large bankers manage to be bailed out by the U.S. Government, others were left holding empty bags of employee promises and struggling to stay afloat.

The current economy

I'm sure I can overwhelm you with data to support my theory. The truth is, by November 2011 reports revealed that there was over 13 million unemployed Americans in the workforce. Thats' over 9% unemployment at a national average.

For minorities such as; African Americans, teenagers and some foreign born Americans, the unemployment rates were over double digits. That entire demographic of workers reported at 10% unemployment and above. Some would argue that overseas markets have contributed to the high unemployment numbers. Others view these numbers as fuel for political debates on unemployment benefits. No matter how you look at it, there's a lot of competition. Its your job to adapt and overcome the employment challenges that's affecting everyone in America.

With all the doom and gloom, economist are still optimistic of our workforce outlook.

One thing I have learned is that recessions are cyclical. They begin and then end, they begin again and then end again.

I have experienced a few recessions and know from experience that they do begin rough and ended slowly at some point over time. I learned a lot of lessons during during those times. I found that prepared professionals have a higher survival percentage in tough times.. Unprepared professionals, seem to buy in to the doom and gloom from the media, and come out in the worst shape. It's no laughing matter when you begin to loose your home, family and job because you didn't have a sustainability plan that could withstand tough times.

Having a job when the recession begins doesn't constitute as a sustainability plan. Your career needs to be in good shape to sustain the tough times if necessary.

Hidden Job Market in todays economy

I recently read an article from a professional who was furious about American entrepreneurs who try hide job opportunities for the public. I wasn't sure how to take that blog but it did peak my interest to read further. Finishing the article, I remembered that I am a "Recovering Recruiter". The hidden job scene is no secret to me. Staffing agencies have been dwelling in that market for centuries.

So, why is he so furious? Its because, the average workforce professional has not paid enough attention to the hidden job market. For example, its estimated that less than 22% of opportunities are advertised. That means, over 78% of the workforce opportunities are hidden to the workforce.

The market has changed and you can credit social media, new technology, and an entire host of other contributors to those stats. The challenge is, getting skilled workers to that other 78% of listings.

What about high income earners? Does this affect them? Yes! This group is affected more than the average professional in the workforce. These are the six figure and above crowd who won't be looking for jobs in the local news paper.

It takes a huge commitment to hire someone who makes over $100,000.00 per year. That means, companies don't want everyone who think they are qualified calling the Personnel Department. Stakeholders looking for this crowd will be looking at every networking avenue available to source the right skills for this big investment. Many of these men and women find themselves out of work longer than those who make less.

High income earners who don't want extended periods of unemployment should focus solely on the hidden market. Less than 8% of high income earners use hidden job searches for employment. Out of the 8%, over 80% of them find jobs. On the other hand, these high earning peers who use the public job board approach, find jobs less than 50% of the time. That's a difference of over 30% in job search success. I don't know about you, but I like the odds a lot better in the hidden job market.

Hidden jobs are opportunities not accessible to the public. These are job listings that are not advertised. They are filled through word of mouth, referrals, social networking and in some cases through clandestine headhunting agreements. (This is the art of recruiting professionals from competitors or similar industry firms for internal jobs not posted to the public)

During the latest recession, The Bureau of Labor Statistics reported over 4 million people being hired each month. During the same time, other reports were showing over 2.4 million jobs were going unfilled.

What does that mean? Unfilled? How can you have unemployment hovering at 10% and over 2.4 million jobs still vacant? The answer is simple, many Americans never saw these jobs open.

The game has changed and you must change as well. Over the last 15 years, I've seen a drastic change in the job market for all professionals. Hidden or not, you have to adjust your approach and be prepared to compete.

Employers are being more selective, candidates are focusing on long-term careers and everyone wants stability. Study this market and develop a game plan for your success.

Rules of engagement

During my service in the United States Army, I learned that there are rules to engagement. These are guidelines of how to successfully fight the battle and win the war.

Today's job seeker must understand that there are two types of professional job hunters; those who are gaining employment and those who are wondering how. Which one are you?

This book will guide you through two phases of becoming employed. The rule is simple. Make finding your next career your business. This book is a tutorial of how to establish the rules of engagement for employment. I have divided the sections in to phases: **Phase 1: Preparation Chapters** and **Phase 2: Execution Chapters.**

Preparation and Execution Chapters

The Preparation Chapters will guide you through the planning stage.

You will complete the Compliance Wheel, personal employability assessment, self evaluation, build a career and academic map. Most people see these chapters as the "Pretty" phases or the "Glamorous" side of job hunting.

The Execution Chapters are considered the ugly side of job searching. I call it **"The Big Ugly"**. These are the blocking and tackling of finding a job. These chapters are guiding the reader through activity, working with recruiters, goal setting, networking, cold calling and interviews.

If you are up to the challenge, lets go to work!

Chapter 1

Child like ambitions
What I want to be when I grow up?

We are innocent and honest as children when it comes to the future. We envision our adulthood while playing with childhood friends. Most of the time, it was just imagining how we would win a battle at the expense of some heroic action toy. I believe we are true to our real passions at an early age, way before we are influenced by media and peer pressure.

Our peers drive the curiosity for social change and create a false sense of reality. In essence, we get out of compliance in life. Our definition of success takes on a new meaning in a world that admires fast wealth and less work.

What do you want to be when you grow up?

How many times did your parents ask, "What do you want to be when you grow up"? Too many times to remember, and the answer probably changed every time.

As a teenager, I remember my mother telling me how special I was and that I'll be an Artist someday. That was easy to determine since I loved to paint. Several days later my grandmother would tell me, "You'll be a doctor". Sure enough, by the end of the week, my aunt would suggest I'd be a lawyer. That's because I enjoyed talking and debating with anyone who would join me.

My family was right in their analogy but failed to realize that helping people was my real passion.

I would play games imagining myself providing solutions to problems using football men, GI-Joe, Cowboys and Indian toys.

As I became an adult, I began to understand my passion for people. It was all about solving problems and helping others. My grandmother and aunt were both right, but my career wasn't to be a doctor or lawyer.

I ended up becoming a recruiter. A professional who helps people find a solution to their employment situation. My family never saw that coming. In fact, I even became an entrepreneur, assisting clients with training, staff and project management solutions. How cool is that?

As young adults, we are influenced by friends, family and fantasy of being successful. These influences transition to our educational decisions and professional direction. Many of us plan to attend certain colleges or obtain employment based on what we "feel" we should be. Others make these decisions based on what is "popular" at the time. The truth is, we should make career decisions based on capabilities and aptitudes; not social peer pressure or financial compensation. I believe your career and academic decisions assist you become compliant with the true destiny for your life. This is the ultimate plan made especially for you.

I look back at those moments in my bedroom, playing out situations of other people's problems and saving the day with the right solution. My imagination wasn't far off from what my natural ability was offering. Fast forward 25 years and I'm living out my childhood dreams. Helping people, running a company and working with some of the brightest people in the world.

I love my job and wake up every morning with a renewed commitment to succeed at my craft. I'm confident that I am in compliance with the plan for my life.

In today's economy many professionals are finding themselves displaced and unsure of what they want to do for the rest of their professional career. The average workforce dynamics for American business changed in the late 90's. This dynamic became even more difficult after the horrendous acts that took place on September 11, 2001.

The workforce as we knew it was no longer the same. Unemployment benefits began to take on a new role. Social Security is no longer a retirement plan and 401K's died in the latest recession. These challenges will test your ability to grow personally and professionally, no matter your background or expertise.

Over the past 10 years, I have met hundreds of professionals who are experiencing a difficult time finding employment in areas they felt qualified for. These are professionals who have spent many years in dead-end jobs outside of their "actual skill set.

Many of them now want to find a quick employment solution. Just a job to get back in the workforce and pay some bills. What kind of future can you have with jobs with little or no sustainability? I often asked myself those questions when coaching a candidate toward a long term career. Then I wonder how happy they would be if they could just find that inner child again, rekindle those attributes discovered while imagining the future.

Then I realize. These are qualified professionals who haven't found their niche in life but have an explanation for not being employed. "What's the problem?" That is the million dollar question I ask during my workshops or coaching a group on career development.

The answers are always the same:

* "No jobs around here".
* "Can't get anyone to give me a chance".
* "All of the good jobs are gone over seas".
* "I can't afford to go back to school for the good jobs".

The problem is not the lack of jobs. The problem is the lack of professionals willing to seek the careers that fit their real expertise. We have to learn to match our natural born talents, loves and passions with opportunities in this great nation.

I have found that no matter what your occupation is, there's someone who has become financially set for life doing it. Just research some of the top Janitorial Service Firms in America. Someone recognized that they enjoyed cleaning and became a multimillionaire doing it. It's not a dirty job to those who enjoy servicing others.

Chapter 2

Unlock your potential for success.
Introduction to the Compliance Wheel

What are the key character traits successful people share? Do you possess them, or have you not unlocked your potential because you haven't focused on them? The answers to those questions will depend on how you view success. If you measure success by having a good job or financial independency, then you may be looking at the wrong traits.

Several yeas ago I began a quest to find out what successful people had that I didn't have. Was I missing the education, or was every successful person just that much smarter than me? I found the answers surveying thousands of candidates who interviewed for jobs while working as a Professional Recruiter for a national consulting firm.

I've interviewed many professionals in my career. A diverse group of men and women who are entrepreneurs, business executives, school teachers, professional athletes, merchants, electricians and even pastors.
The list would go on for days of every skill set and personality I've interviewed over my career.

What I found was surprising. It wasn't some special human trait that made them successful.

It was a compilation of non-tangible traits that each successful professional shared. Those traits could be categorized in to four groups. I called it the **Compliance Wheel.**

Why Compliance Wheel? Because, I used the automobile tire as the connection. When you have 4 brand new tires, your car runs like it is on glass. Your ride experience increases and you enjoy taking long trips in total comfort. However, when one of those tires begin to deflate or is damaged, your riding experience decreases and you begin to limit your trips or take short cuts. What do you do when your tire isn't compliant with OEM regulations for tread wear or air pressure? You make a change.

My survey results were much deeper than the usual motivational jargon you get for success. There were areas in which you could not deny as God given talent. Industry research can provide you with a laundry list of traits such as, hard working, proper education, dedication and skill. Although, all of those characteristics are vital, I found these individuals felt successful when their purpose, passion, attitude and spirit were all in sync. Very similar to our automobile tire scenario. When the four areas were working together for one common cause, the travel experience was much smoother.

I've developed the Compliance Wheel using these 4 key focus areas. The Compliance Wheel can be applied professionally and personally to unlock your potential. Contrary to what most people believe, your success is defined by being compliant with all aspects of your life. To find out, you can ask yourself simple questions.
Questions like, is your struggle continuous because you refuse to follow your passion? Are you striving for success in areas that don't represent who you are?

What is Success?

My definition of success is simple. Success is when your Purpose, Passion, Attitude and Spirit are synchronized. You begin to see life different because you have a purpose.

You understand exactly what you want out of life and that fuels your passion to achieve more. Success begins to come naturally because your attitude exudes a positive outlook. While others are focusing on doom and gloom, you believe that life has more to offer you. Your spirit becomes contagious and you find others more excited to be around you.

The truth is, what makes you successful doesn't define your success. That's where the society has misled our business community. Not everyone was built to be entrepreneurs, so why does our society place a premium on men and women who are business owners? They are no more successful than the Chemist who works for a major pharmaceutical firm.

I have helped people unlock their true potential by using the Compliance Wheel during interviews. One interviewee discovered that her real passion was teaching.

Throughout the Compliance Wheel process, she learned that her challenge with finding sustainable work was because she didn't like her current career field. Her only focus was to maintain a certain lifestyle driven by financial gains. This candidate felt that she could obtain her financial goals being a teacher.

Just like thousands of other professionals in the market, my interviewee was in denial and has been in and out of dead end jobs her entire career. Unless she takes the time to evaluate where her professional career is and where it is going, she will continue to have short term success.

The Compliance Wheel

Every successful person strives to get better at what they do.

They are self motivated and build great habits around their documented goals. The Compliance Wheel is your personal assessment process. Throughout this chapter, you will identify your strategic plan and create some excellent habits that will lead you to success. Make sure you tune out the naysayers and tune in your own intuition.

The 4 areas of concentration will eliminate doubt and guide you toward making better decisions for a better career. Let's get started by getting a better understanding of the 4 quadrants.

*Purpose
*Passion
*Attitude
*Spirit

A. **Purpose Quadrant** = This focus area is all about getting in touch with yourself. No matter who you are or how much you have accomplished, you must have a purpose. Your true purpose is the reason you exist in life. Its what you are designed to do. Finding your purpose can open up your mind to endless opportunities using areas that are aligned with your life mission, vision and values. Your purpose is the strategic plan. It outlines where you are, what you do and why you work so hard to achieve your goals. It is the foundation for a happy life and a key ingredient for success.

B. **Passion Quadrant** = Everyone is driven by something. Your passion is the energy source that ensures your goals are achieved. I believe the passion fuels your purpose and attitude through times of uncertainty. For most of us, it takes a difficult challenge to unlock that passion, but successful people feed on it daily. You will need to find that passion. These exercises will help you build your passions for the things that mean the most to you.

C. **Attitude Quadrant** = Attitude is everything! Without the right attitude, you can't endure the ups and downs of personal and professional strife. It is the "fight for your success but embrace your failures" attitude that determines your definition of success. There is power in your attitude when you find the bright spot in every situation.

You will learn to change your habits that mold your attitude. Training your mind to be more positive when you have reason not to be.

D. **Spiritual Quadrant** = Your internal faith system is the "I BELIEVE" contribution to your attitude quadrant. Therefore, why not begin with believing in yourself. In my experience, I've found that most people fail because they don't believe they can succeed. Creating a loosing spirit can effect your purpose, passion and attitude. Your spirit is what keeps you engaged. It can be the only factor that motivates you to press forward, or it can be the depressant that keeps you on the couch.

The Spirit Quadrant will help you channel your spirit toward wisdom, knowledge, faith and better quality of life. Now say, "I BELIEVE I CAN DO ANYTHING I SET MY MIND TO DO"!.

* Purpose

The act of establishing your real professional purpose is developing a direction for your life. You have to reveal key aspects about yourself and what you feel your purpose in life is. The Purpose Quadrant becomes your Mission Statement.

I think we were all born with a purpose to fulfill and if you are not living within your purpose, life can be a little more difficult. The same principle applies with your professional career. If you don't discover your professional purpose, you may find yourself in a dead end jobs with no career outlook.

To discover your professional purpose, you have to spend some time conducting self evaluations. The evaluations explore areas of your God given talent to determine where you can contribute your career path efforts. In fact, once you have begun to build a strong foundation, you will continue to evaluate your professional purpose for the rest of your life. This keeps your plan innovative and ensures that you never end up in a career roadblock. All you need to do is schedule some time each quarter to review and assess where you are according to your professional purpose.

Personal Purpose Parallel

Does your professional purpose connect with your personal ambition? Absolutely! As you evaluate yourself, you will ask questions that identify your personal inner feelings, loves, likes and dislikes. Your own answers will provide a snapshot of your true loves in life.

Keep in mind that your true purpose may not be what you had in mind for yourself. However, to be happy and in sync with your Compliance Wheel, you must make some tough decisions on how you plan to progress through life. You will need to visualize where you are and where you want to be.

For instance, I interviewed a graduate from a prestigious university about 10 years ago who had written several books and articles about technology.

He had been in and out of jobs within the I.T. field and couldn't attain sustainability in the workforce. During my interview, I asked him why didn't he just focus on writing since it seemed more like his passion in life? His answer was candid. He didn't think there was enough money in writing to support his projected lifestyle.

That example was an eye opener for me. Here is a man who was highly educated, but so far from his professional purpose. I am quite convinced that he could have gone on to be an award winning author, career curriculum developer, or even a collegiate professor.

What he didn't realize was, once you are in compliance with your professional purpose, you can have any lifestyle you want. Your expertise will be exemplary because you're doing what you love. The rewards are endless when you have passion and purpose in your professional life.

How to discover my purpose?

To help find your real professional purpose, ask yourself the following questions. Be honest with yourself and take some time to write out your answers. Use a separate sheet of paper if needed.

Task #1

Your Purpose question	Your "true" Purpose
1. Can you currently identify your purpose in life?	
2. Name one thing you was born to be?	
3. What would you do if asked to do one thing for the rest of your life?	
4. What do you enjoy learning about?	
5. What do you enjoy the most about your current profession?	
6. What do your peers say you're best at?	
7. What did you want to be as a child?	
8. What is your favorite attribute?	

Task #2

Now lets dig a little deeper.

* Take about 30 minutes and find a quite room. Write down all the things you like or love to do. Include your professional likes and loves.
* Close your eyes and meditate a while.
* Visualize your career path, life status and future goals.
* See if they match up with what you thought your purpose in life was.
* Also, compare them to your career path. If they don't match, then you are off track. If they do, then you are on your way to a great professional and personal journey once you put it all together.

Personal Purpose: (Write it down)

_____

_____

_____

_____

_____

_____

_____

Professional Purpose: (Write it down)

_____

_____

_____

_____

_____

_____

* Passion

Some scholars believe that if you find your passions in life it will connect your purpose. That could very well be the case. I think we all agree that the two are truly connected to each other in some fashion.

One of my business partners firmly believes that discovering your passion will drive your purpose. I see that first hand with him. He spent 10 years in the National Football League (NFL) and has been coaching football since his retirement in 2007. I have had the pleasure of watching him coach and it is obvious how he inspires young men to win.

People are inspired by passionate people. When you are passionate about something, it seems like you are going the extra mile. In fact, all you are doing is taking additional steps toward something you love to do. I know professionals who hate passionate people who win. They believe these type of people are just over the top personalities who are annoying. It's hard to be around someone like that and it could rub off on you. My daughters call them "Haters", but I see them as sad souls who have never found their passion for life. These people find your passion outrageous, but successful people find it contagious. That is why you see successful professionals associated with other successful professionals. They feed on each other. It's just like the slogan my oldest daughter came up with, "Success is a package, it comes with Haters".

Is your brand personality passionate?

Are you living your passion? Does your professional career connect your passions in life? What is your employability brand personality? Yes, you have an employability brand character. Is it one that shows passion or depression?

People can identify your professional passion through your verbal and nonverbal actions. Recruiters are experts at reading through the fluff and seeing your actual employment personality.

As you start your professional career you will create your employability brand. This is how employers can tell if you love what you do or just going through the motions of life.

Many professionals in the workforce are just going through the motions. These are "Check Collectors". Employees who are miserable most of the time, collecting a paycheck and hating everyone who is successful at the worksite.

Managers and recruiters can see them from a mile away. You may slip through the recruiting process but you will be identified when it comes down to your annual evaluation. You have to ask yourself honestly, are you a Check Collector or a Rain Maker? Which employee are you?

Now lets get passionate!

No Purpose in life has a chance to succeed if it isn't fueled by passion. Your true success can be driven by an energy to achieve it. It's the fuel of your purpose. Your passion allows you to accept challenges while staying focused on your goals. You can't achieve a sustainable professional life if you don't care about what you do.

I tell my students that this process of being passionate is very similar to dating. Those who don't care about their mate will always look for ways to get out of the relationship. Job seekers who can't find their passion will spend most of their time alone or in transition. Looking for greener pastures? Are you in transition a lot? Are you moving from job to job? Are you getting interviews but not getting offers?

Your employability brand is probably showing managers that you are not passionate about your career. Check you passion levels.

Begin to uncover what you are passionate about by answering these basic eight questions. Use additional paper and ask more self evaluating questions if necessary. Again, the key is to be honest and dive in to what drives you!

Your Passion question	What do you have a Passion for?
1. What are you most passionate about?	
2. Are you achieving your dreams?	
3. If you were given one choice to do something special in life, what would you fight for?	
4. List one thing you wish you would've never given up on.	
5. What does your friends say you're most passionate about?	
6. Name one area you may have lost a passion for in your current job.	
7. When was the last time you felt passionate about your career?	

Your Passion question	What do you have a Passion for?
8. Name one thing you would passionately do without pay.	

* Attitude

Everyone has heard the old expression, "Attitude is everything". Today with so many Americans in transition your attitude may affect how long you remain unemployed.

We can all agree that it can be extremely difficult to maintain a positive attitude when your future doesn't look so bright. You probably are asking yourself "Why now?" or "How am I going to get through this?".

Being caught in transition is extraordinarily difficult. It's a life changing event that can have an impact on your attitude. The first thing you need to do is get over the fact that you are in transition. Next, is stop blaming yourself or others for your unfortunate incident. Embrace your situation and begin to piece your life back together.

You start with upgrading your attitude. Move on to the next chapter in your life, and allow your passions and purpose to be fulfilled. Pursue your goals in life no matter how late in the game it may be. Develop a short-term memory and coach yourself up. Meaning, your attitude probably needs to be improved to persevere through your career development process.

Where is my attitude now?

A positive attitude will deliver your next job a lot faster than exuding a looser attitude.

Employers want to hire those who add value within their work environment. Your attitude weighs high on the employment matrix for the opportunity.

A positive attitude reassures prospective employers that they are making the right professional and financial commitment. At the end of the day, no employer wants to be stuck paying a negative employee.

Types of attitudes

There are various scientific forms of attitudes a person can have. However, I believe you can distribute them in to four main categories. You have positive, negative, judgement and content attitudes.

The Positive = He or she always look for positive outcomes in life. They always seem to find themselves blessed with opportunities and don't fear failure. They know that failure is a part of life.

Negative = Some may think this is the worst attitude of the four but it's not. A negative attitude will never progress because they don't find it necessary to put all that work in to a failing cause. These are the play it safe guys, people who watch you fail and then attack your choice for trying. These are the naysayers in your life who want to see you fail.

Judgement = Now here is the attitude of choice for most people. This is the attitude that reminds you of your short comings. The "I told you so" and the "you should have never done that" crowd. These are the easiest attitudes to deal with in my opinion. They are not the most damaging of the four attitudes if you can just handle the constant reminders when communicating.

Contentment = To me, this is the worst of the four attitudes. This is the attitude that keeps exceptional talent in the closet. Too many times have we seen individuals with immense potential fall waste due to a contentment attitude.
This attitude can paralyze a person if they get stuck in a bad scenario. It is extremely difficult to overcome if you lack the drive to succeed. Stay away from this one. It can cripple you.

This exercise is designed to identify challenges in your life (professional & personal) in which your attitude allowed you to overcome a challenge.

Document 2 scenarios in which your attitude was the reason you failed.

Negative Scenario #1

_____
_____
_____

Negative Scenario #2

_____
_____
_____

Now document 2 scenarios in which your attitude was the reason you succeeded.

Scenario #3

_____
_____
_____

Scenario #4

_____

_____

_____

***This exercise can unlock your potential to become successful by answering some key questions regarding your personal attitude. Take these quick questions and apply them to your failure scenarios. Answer them honestly and look for the following:

a. Why didn't I do things differently?
b. Who really was the blame for my failures?
c. How much control did I have in the outcome?
d. Was it really worth going through the fuss?
e. How much would I give to do it all again?
f. Who did I hurt in the end?

Attitude can be a way of life, social perception, self concept and a learned behavior over a course of time. You can improve your attitude by learning new behaviors. Therefore, your attitude can influence the level of your professional success and personal satisfaction.

* Spirit

Job hunting can put you in the wrong frame of mind. Failure to find employment within a short amount of time can affect how you feel, act and respond to your tasks. You begin to gather negative thoughts and find excuses for your unemployment.

There is good news for those who struggle in this area. You can manage your spiritual outlook within your job search. The trick is making it a priority. Focusing on high energy thoughts over watching the local news. Read more career based books vs. the dark depressing media.

Redirecting your thoughts will put you in the right spirit for employment searches.

One thing to keep in mind, recruiters love high spirited candidates. The majority of the hiring managers you will meet can identify high spirited candidates over the low depressed ones. Human Resources, hiring managers and recruiters see you as an investment for long term needs. This investment must have the right frame of mind during good and bad economic times. They want to know if you can be a good teammate or workplace cancer when times get tough.

Big brother took my job!

I have a dear friend who found herself unemployed. She was the victim of a down economy. This placed her amongst millions of Americans who were in transition or displaced during the latest recession.

I checked in with her to see how she was doing in her job search and was taken a back with her demeanor. My friend was typically cheerful with high energy and a loving spirit. However, this time she was totally deflated.

I asked her how the search was going and she began to tell me a terribly long story. Her tale was of "The Man", who wanted her out of a job.

Then she continued to share how there was no jobs in America because "the immigrants have them all". It was obvious that my friend had become depressed analyzing circumstances that are out of her control.

My friend fell in to a depressed state by convincing herself that she'll never find employment. Every job opportunity she pursued, employers showed no interest.

I informed her that there would be no interest if she entered the interview with a "probably not me" spirit. She was loosing the job before getting started.

Know and understand that you are in a different place in life. Remind yourself that there is a job out there for you. **NEVER GIVE UP!** Create a spiritual journal and log in positive things about yourself or your professional expertise. While you are journaling everything positive, developing a positive mantra for your new quest. Above everything else, forgive yourself for giving up on your goals so soon. Don't dwell on your short comings. Focus on how happy you'll be once you land your next job. Believe you'll find the next job today. Know it and have faith!

Is my spirit attractive to employers?

Yes, employers are attracted to people with a great spirit. Take a look at your resume. Good recruiters can spot candidates who have a dark spirit. If you wrote your resume during a depressing state, your resume will probably read depressingly mundane. That's not too hard to identify.

Interviews are no different from depressing candidates who submit bland resume. You have one shot to knock the ball out of the park and you have no room for your B-Game. Never interview outside of your successful spirit (A-Game). Get upbeat before you meet your next employer. I always suggest that my candidates exercise a few hours before your interview. That seems to kick up the drive and creativity in some candidates.

Another tip that works for me is listening to your favorite song right before the big meeting. That one seems to work wonders when your not at your best. Whatever you do, don't interview with a losing spirit. You might not know which spirit you are exuding, but everyone around you knows.

Where is my spirit?
- Do you wake up in the morning to find yourself afraid of failing?
- Are you going through the motions of life because you lost faith in your ability to achieve your goals?
- Do you base your decisions on the potential of a negative outcome?
- Are you unconditionally faithful in your quest for success?
- How much faith do you have in yourself?

To achieve success, you must have a keen understanding of what feeds your spirit for success. I believe that you are the CEO of Your success. It's up to you to make active your inner spirit. Your inner spirit attracts either negative or positive events in your life. I have found that there are things you can do to promote the habit of increasing your successful spirit and decreasing your spirit of failure.

Here are some tips for you to include in your daily, weekly and monthly tasks that can help you with being successful.

1. **Change your negative lifestyle to a positive one.**
   a. Separate yourself from negative people.
   b. Focus on positive meditation when you are alone.
   c. Speak positive things in to your life.
   d. Eat healthy

2. **Find something to Inspire you.**
   a. Take a moment of inspiration from your life and use it daily.
   b. Read a motivational book once a month for 6 months.
   c. Find pride in everything you do.
   d. Write down obtainable goals.

3. Recruit a Mentor.
    a. Find a person with a positive spirit to mentor you.
    b. Try to find someone at work to mentor you professionally.

4. Do something physical each day.
    a. Take a walk or a jog to jump start your mind.
    b. Try to work out if possible. It helps you mentally and keeps you looking fit physically.

5. Read something positive or motivational
    a. Read a religious passage, meditate or even pray.
    b. Find other spiritually refreshing books to read.
    c. Attend motivational speaking engagements.
    d. Buy motivational books on tape or CD.

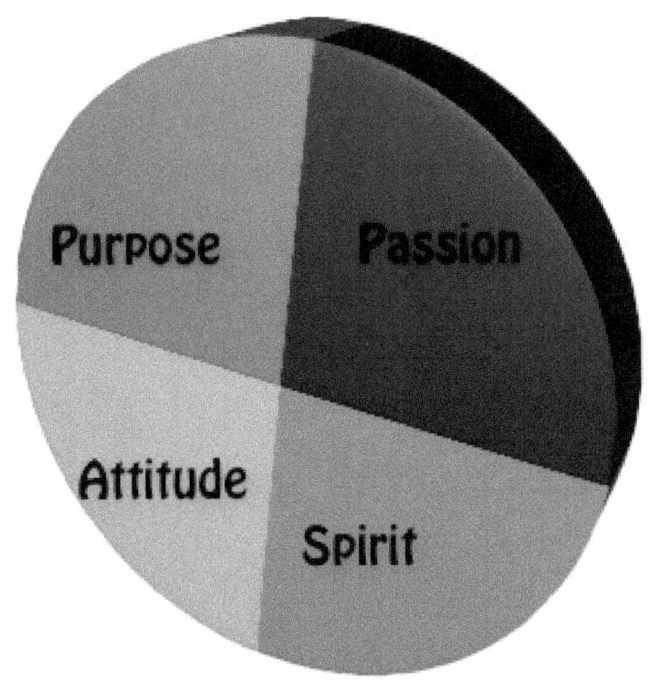

Compliance Wheel Summary

Where are you now in your life? Are you in Compliance?
You can always tell the person who is in compliance by the
way they live their life. These are individuals who:

* Are in tune with their passions, purpose and have the right
  attitude.
* Most importantly, they have a beautiful spirit that attracts
  others to them.
* They are very focused.
* They don't loose site of their personal and professional
  goals.
* They don't get detoured by set backs.
* They believe they are born for something greater than
  themselves.
* They love what they do.
* They are inspired by themselves and others.
* They have the best attitude in all situations.

Make sure that you connect your Purpose, Passion, Attitude
and Spirit. There are plenty of articles on the web discussing
how some people find their compliance during these difficult
times. For some it will take bad circumstances to recognize
them, for others it could be a planned process.

Chapter 3

Are you employable?
What is your personal employability?

Your journey toward employment hinges on your personal employability. Finding employment goes beyond making normal calls, google searches and establishing an award winning resume. Employment begins with the process of self assessments to better understand your employment skills. What are your true strengths and weaknesses?

During the your employment search, it's crucial to communicate your skill set to your prospective employer. He/she will be looking for key indicators on your resume or during the interview process that will meet their immediate need.

Your skills can be divided in to three categories:

Core Skills: These are skills that are a direct reflection of your values, morals and ethics. Could also include your personal traits and characteristics.

Transferable Skills: Personal or Professional talents that can be translated in to employable skills throughout your career.

Applied (Acquired) Skills: Skills learned through education, training, or employment based skills acquired over time.

Core Skills

Exercise One: Using a separate sheet of paper or your book, develop a list of your **Core Skills**. Once you have done that, select 5 that best describe you. Use the list below to assist with developing your top 5 core skills. You may search the internet for additional cores skills to include on your list.

Caring	Appreciative	Patient
Advising	Flexible	Punctual
Reliable	Loyal	Mature
Optimistic	Active	Honest
Eager	Intuitive	Businesslike
Effective	Adept	Friendly
Innovative	Meticulous	Organized
Firm	Courageous	Dynamic
Insightful	Disciplined	Authentic

Top Core Skills

1	
2	
3	
4	
5	

Transferable Skills

Exercise Two: Using a separate sheet of paper or your book, develop a list of your **Transferable Skills.** Once you have done that, select 5 that best describe you. Use the list below to assist you with developing your top 5 transferable skills.

Computer literacy
Team Player
Supervise others
Use my hands
Repair things
Writer
Results driven
Print by hand
Operate equipment
Multitask
Detailed
expertise
Enjoy Math

Problem solving
Ability to delegate
Audit records
Organize people
Increase sales
Typing
Meet deadlines
Handle complaint
Plan agenda
Research
Budget
Collect Funds

Top Transferable Skills

1	
2	
3	
4	
5	

Applied Skills

<u>Exercise Three:</u> Using a separate sheet of paper of your book, develop a list of your **Applied Skills**. Once you have done that, select 5 that best describe you. Use the list below to assist you with developing your top 5 Applied skills.

Certifications	Education level
OJT	Life Experience
Military Service	Politics
Authored books	Social service
Projects Intelligence exp.	Memberships
Training	Drafting
Forecasting	Bookkeeping

Top Applied Skills

1	
2	
3	
4	
5	

Lets see how employable you are now?

Honestly complete the exercises, you'll get one step closer to knowing if you're applying your skills in the right place. Job seekers who falsify their expertise have a habit of finding short-term employment instead of long-term careers.

Let's begin with the only person who can have an impact on your career. YOU! You have to make sure that your current skills are employable in your target industry. It makes no sense if you are targeting an Accounting position and have no interest in math. This is a common mistake made by professionals who seek employment in the wrong field of expertise. This can also be a costly mistake that can prolong unemployment over the course of your work life.

Self Assessment

Understanding your employability can be exciting as you discover your true abilities and new career ventures. Lets continue to dive down in to your self assessment for a better view of your employability. This next exercise is designed to promote open dialog on how employers perceive you. I call it the "what recruiters will not tell you section".

During my tenure in the recruiting business, there was several times I would have to pull a candidate aside and ask some real personal questions. As a Professional Recruiter, I felt it was my job to help the candidate, if I was going to represent them to my employers. Some of my assessments were well received and others were not.

Honesty was the best attribute when trying to help my clients. That principle allowed me to help those who didn't understand the art of finding employment.

What I found over the years, was that being honest with your candidates allowed them the opportunity to get better. It's the evaluation process as they were looking for my agency to help them get employed.

Tip: The person who holds him or herself accountable through honest assessments achieve success more often that those who do not. No matter if it is internal or external, self assessments are vital for your career growth.

My personal employability assessment

I have compiled a questionnaire to help you understand your personal employability. The key is "HONESTY". Complete the exercise by answering the questions asked below. Feel free to have someone give you their honest opinion of your skills.

Fill in the blanks to self assess your employability. If you need more space, use a notebook or blank sheets of paper to complete. Try not to use "Yes and "No" answers when filling out your responses. Spend time with yourself and be more qualitative in your response.

Employability Questionnaire

1. Can I communicate my skills professionally? Why or why not?

2. Can I elaborate on the skills listed on my resume?

3. Does my resume "best" describe my actual skills? Why not?

4. Does my education match the level of opportunities I am pursuing?
   a. If so, explain where your strong points.
   b. If not, explain your plan to correct it.

---

5. Did I actually do the things listed on my resume?
   a. If so, highlight your major accomplishments.
   b. If not, what areas should your remove?

6. Am I a "Jack of all trades and master of none"?
   a. If so, what can I delete from my resume to eliminate that stereotype?
   b. If not, what skills listed have no relevance in my career?

7. Does my work experience reflect my salary request?

8. Am I really a team player or do I work best alone?

9. Is leadership my best quality or am I better in a support role?
   a. List your leadership roles on your resume:
   b. List your best support roles on your resume:

10. Are my Core Skills my biggest assets? If so, which ones?

11.Which Transferable Skills will allow me to be "great" during my interview?
   a. Are they currently on your resume?
   b. Are they hidden within the fluff or in plain sight?
   c. Which ones directly affect your employability?

12. Does my Applied Skills and work experience fit my current geographical market? (Your current City or Regional Employability)

13. Do I look professional in my business attire?
   a. How do I describe my business attire? (Youthful, Mature, Business, Church or Casual)
   b. Take down an inventory of the business attire have's and needs.

14. Do I need to work on my personal fitness and hygiene?
   a. What area do I need to focus on?
   b. What is my strategy for getting it done during my
      employment search?

15. Do I smoke Cigarettes?
   a. Has anyone ever asked me if I smoke in an interview?
   b. Do I smoke before interviews?

16. Describe your communication skills. Is it professional,
   casual or social?

17. Do I need to get more education?
   a. What level of education will benefit me?
   b. Do I just need a refresher course?
   c. Does my target job require vocational training?

18. Am I choosing this career path because I love the daily
   employment activities, or because I can make more
   money if hired?

19. Are you willing to work two jobs until you get on your
   feet?

20. Lastly, do I have the right Purpose, Passion, Attitude and
   Spirit for employment? Explain why you do or do not.

Industry Assessment

Are you targeting the right industry? Does your target
market hire employees with your background?   Maybe your
current region is not so rewarding for your employment
search. These are all excellent questions you can ask
yourself while assessing your employability. It is just as
important as the 20 questions you completed earlier.

It reminds me of a situation I encountered back while speaking in a rural town of South Carolina. This town was ravished with disparity and economic challenges, but I was enthusiastic to educate them on opportunities outside of the manufacturing market.

As I began to conclude my speech, I asked for closing questions to ensure that everyone understood my message on vocational training. That is when reality set for most of the attendees. Most of them asked me if I thought there was a need for technology in their region. Based on the question, I would say that the majority of them had already taken computer courses at the local college. I would also bet that the majority of the attendees who took those computer classes were coached in to the course enrollment. It's easy to get coached in to taking computer classes when you're told its the future of job security. The problem was, technology isn't a major characteristic for that small town. They were in the middle of a manufacturing region with very little technology firms. I felt compelled to be honest, so I informed them of their choices:

Options:
1. Prepare to travel to the nearest technology region where there is more technical based employers or
2. Move to a more progressive market that provides a competitive advantage for employees with your skills.

Options #1 & #2 were not popular options for many of the attendees, because of their commitment to live out their lives in the same town they were born in. This is exactly why you must have a better understanding of your skill market and its geographical impact on your employment security.

I have provided some resources you can use to determine your competitiveness within your home town or region. Research your expertise and background to make sure they fit your geographical make up.

Resource	Location	Information
Chamber of Commerce	Your local City/Town www.uschamber.com	Professional make up of your region. To include businesses, trades, industries and individual information for movers and shakers in your city.
Workforce Development Board	Your Local workforce entity: Employment Commission, Unemployment office,	Provide you with who is hiring, what industry and skills needed to fulfill the job needs.
Business Journals	Your local City/Region has a Business Journal.	Detailed information on industries, companies and economic outlook for your local region.
County Government Services Site	Your Local County Federal or State website.	Information on living in the area, doing business in the area and recreational/ culture for the market.
Business Journal Book of List	Your Local Business Journal post a annual "Book of Lis". You can purchase for less than $50.00.	Scope of every major organization within your region. Outlines to employers, industries, executives, sports and healthcare information. It is one of the most utilized marketing media amongst business and sales professionals.

What is a geographical characteristic

The recent economic downturn is the main reason we all must focus on the geographical aspects unemployment. In late 2007 and early 2008, the economy began to slow down. Major lay offs and plant closings throughout America was the sign of a hard felt economic collapse. America was hit hard. What professionals in the workforce noticed was the influx of individuals who were becoming displaced. Professionals with no idea of what to do next. I called them the "lost souls" of the job market. These were the individuals who moved to a location, became displaced but refuse to relocate to sustainable markets for their skill set.

Bad example
I met a Software Developer who moved to Charlotte, NC during the height of the computer boom. He and his family had moved from Washington, DC and was excited to meet someone else who had made the same journey. His background was not necessarily financial applications, but cyber security. He had taken a job at one of the financial institutions which was looking for someone with his expertise. He was sold on the schools, weather and the allure of Charlotte's growth. Several months later, he contacted me looking for employment but refused to move back to the D.C. market. Unfortunately, over the next several years, he lost his security clearance and was forced to taking a lesser paying job outside of his skill set. This new opportunity kept him in the market but making half the salary he needed to keep up his lifestyle. He loved Charlotte more than his career and paid dearly for it.

Good example
I have a young family member who majored in Computer Information Technology. As he was continuing to get his masters degree in Information Systems, he kept the corporate world at the top of his priority list. He was a willing volunteer for internships throughout the U.S..

These internships were with leading organizations that would eventually offer him opportunities once he graduated from college. The only problem was the offers were all in the Midwest. None of them were close to home and moving away from the East Coast was going to be an uncomfortable decision for him.

After graduating with his masters degree, there were no offers close to his hometown. He knew he had to make that tough decision. **Decision 1)** Stay on the East Coast and continue to search for employment. **Decision 2)** Take an opportunity in the Midwest performing duties that would boost his career.

He made Decision #2, moved to Iowa and lived there for five years. His tough decision finally paid off when the market had a demand for his new skills earned in Iowa.

Did he ever make it back to the East Coast? Yes, and is currently in a better role, with higher income and glad he made the Decision #2.

Those example may seem extreme from one end to the other but it is particularly common in todays workforce. Professionals are making moving decisions to new cities without researching the professional outlook.

Tip:
Don't marry your geographical location! Focus on identifying the market that best suit your career path. If you are not looking to reinvent yourself professionally, then look to create a relocation strategy to enhance your employability.

If you are a welder in a banking town, your sustainability is not as good as the Accountant or Bank Teller would be. Find a manufacturing town that would have a greater demand for your skills. Make the move and watch your employability increase over time.

Here are some questions that will help you understand your current employability. These questions can also help you if you are considering a career move or transitioning to a new market.

Industry Employability Questionnaire

1. Where are the jobs for my background?
2. Did I review the local employment outlook report?
3. Who are the largest employers in my market?
4. What is the makeup of my current region?
   a. Manufacturing
   b. Banking
   c. Energy
   d. Telecommunications or Information Technology
   e. Defense/Government
5. If I am terminated today, are my skills in demand in this market?
6. Am I prepared to move if needed to continue my career?
7. What obstacles are keeping me from making the right geographical move for my career.
   a. Family ties
   b. Money
   c. Transportation
   d. Fear
8. Am I living in the right employment market?

Your employability is a direct reflection of your career choices. You are responsible for your ability to become employed and maintain employment. It seems harsh but as professionals, that is your number one job.

This means that we all have a perpetual process of career development. It can be as smooth at you want or it can end before you expect it. Regardless of how you view this process, it never ends until retirement.

Tip:
Couple of additional key critical thinking questions while evaluating your next job:

* What does this role do for my career path progression?
* If I was terminated within the next 90 days, what skills would I have developed that could advance my career further?
* Is this a stepping stone, lateral movement or a waste of time?

Do not let your fears keep you away from experiencing new markets. You should think like an entrepreneur and look for ways to make yourself better. You will become more attractive to the decision makers who will invest in your brand. When you lose your commitment to improve, you lose your competitiveness. Lack of competitiveness will lead toward unhealthy habits and complacent career attitude.

Chapter 4

Career Mapping
Why is Career Mapping important?

What is a Career Map? A Career Map is a professional business plan that outlines your current status. It is the big picture approach to your professional development. Career Maps outline your action plan and includes short and long-term milestones. Your personal Career Map breaks down all of your career strategies. It helps keep you focused on all of your professional options, as you work though the milestones over time.

Developing your Personal Career Map is "THE" most important process to begin your new career. This action plan will eventually become your road map to success. It begins with your self assessment (which you did in Chapter 2) and including process tools such as:

---

*Setting goals
* Researching markets
* Gathering information about your industry
* Developing new skills (Educational Plan)
* Change Management (making jobs to advance)
* Understanding your realities as well as,
* Occupational performance measurements (evaluating how you perform in each role)

There is no specific template for establishing a successful Career Map. Remember to be honest as you explore occupations, expand your education and identify new opportunities.

Career Maps need to have the following:

1. **Your beginning and end goals:** You have to begin with a goal. Some career plans have several goals that are in alignment with milestones. The key is knowing where you want to end while establishing where you begin. Start with the end in mind.
2. **Action Items:** These are marching steps in which you will accomplish your tasks. Each action item will be connected to your milestones. They can include task such as: internships, volunteer, job roles, experience, project types etc.
3. **Timeframe:** How long will it take to accomplish my goal? Some Career Goals will dictate the timeframe. Be patient. Keep in mind that the further out you set your milestones the more focus you must be to obtain them. Most people wash out of their plan because they didn't set obtainable goals.
4. **Education:** Your professional education is a direct reflection of your career advancement. Establishing an Educational Map that mirrors your Career Plan is critical to realistic career goals.
5. **Milestones:** Your Career Map will have achievement milestones. These are action items that will keep you engaged and on track to your career success. They also are measurable in your evaluation process. They also reflect your hard work and determination to achieve your ultimate goal. The more milestones you reach the closer you are to success.

Things to avoid while developing your Career Map

* **Advice from unqualified coaches:** Keep in mind that not all successful people understand how to coach you in your professional development process. Don't take advice from those who are not qualified to give you career advice.
* **Financial Initiatives:** Anything that begins with money first is probably not going to work out for you in the long run. Financial rewards should be a consideration but not the major motivation. Always ask yourself, "would you do this job for free"?
* **Fearful decision:** Don't be afraid to take some professional risks. Risk is part of personal and professional development. There are not too many decisions you'll make as an adult that doesn't involve some form of risk. Make a calculated decision, supported with research and confidence. Fearful professionals typically finish last.
* **Naysayers:** Keep clear of negative people. Anyone who is willing to criticize you for advancing your career, probably doesn't want you to leave them behind. Avoid the Naysayers the most!
* **Geographical infatuations:** Keep in mind that some professionals are required to relocate at least once in their careers. Some organizations even include relocation as part of their progression progress. Educate your family members on your Career Map and relocation expectations in the beginning. Come to an agreement and be prepared when the time comes. It will make your professional decision a lot easier.

***If possible, you want to find a mentor in your target industry. Someone who can assist you with developing a realistic goal, timeframe and obtainable milestones. This will expedite your research and help you develop a professional reference throughout your career.

Here is an example of an entry-level technicians Career Map. Your assignment is to develop your career progression outline based on your new professional goals.

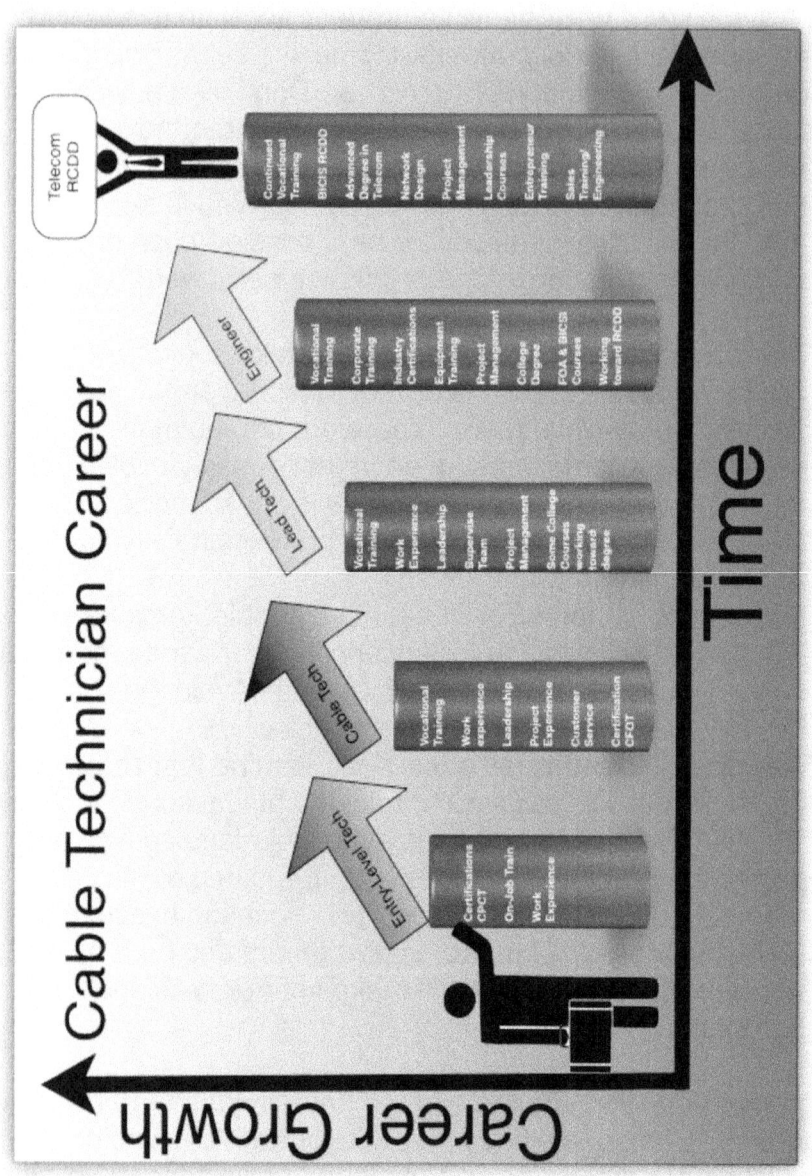

Training Plan

Training Plans are professional tools that outline your academic growth in accordance to your career strategy. To comply with the guidelines set from your career map, your training strategy must include topics such as:

* High School Diploma or G.E.D.
* Vocational Training or Trade School
* Certificate Programs
* Accredited Certifications/Credentials
* Institutions of Higher Learning
* Associate Degrees
* Advanced Degree Programs
* On the job training

As illustrated in the Career Map example, you can see how your career begins to grow as you develop as a professional. Part of that development is continued education. In the Career Growth graph, you can see the Telecom Technician's wants to become an Sr. Engineer. To achieve these goals, you must have a training strategy to get you there.

Continued Education

I have learned how valuable continued education is while serving as an Executive Officer for two small businesses. I discovered that continued education is an absolute must if you want to stay competitive in today's market. Trying to stay ahead of your competition without the proper knowledge can stall your business progress. This lack of academic priority can land you in the unemployment line.

Can you think of a more challenging time than now to begin a new career without the proper trade knowledge?

During your self assessment, did you ask yourself if you currently possess the academic tools to get your career and keep it advancing? Does your career match your academic expertise? Can you connect your education with your projected Career Map?

So, how do we connect education with your Career Map? Easy, your Training Plan works along side your Career Map serving as a tool to keep you on pace with your professional goals. It should be strategic in plan, but focused on goals identified in the Career Map. In the next diagram you will see how a Cable Technician planned both the career and education during the same session. I'm sure the strategic plan was set for each milestone and an educational goal was established at the same time. This type of strategy will keep our Technician on a good pace every step of the way.

How do I fund my academic goals?

Funding your education isn't always an easy task. Again, nothing in life worth having isn't without some challenge. It just requires a little patience.

I've coached mature professionals on training plans and was shocked to hear how many did not know how to finance their training needs. Spending a little time on the phones and researching the internet will uncover many training opportunities and ways to fund them.

In some cases, funding could be as simple as qualifying and others you may need a sponsor. I have even seen candidates interview for a scholarship and receive over $6,000 of training at no cost. In any case, you have to conduct the research and uncover opportunities to support your goals.

Training Funding Sources

1. **Scholarships:** Some vocational schools and most colleges offer scholarships for those who qualify. Scholarships can be based on performance, minority status or a variation of other factors. Ask your academic provider for information on all of their scholarships.
2. **Grants:** Community associations and nonprofit organizations could be a great source for grants. Universities also have grants available based on the grantor's criteria. Check with your training provider to make sure you don't miss out on grant funding for your education.
3. **Military Service:** If you have served in the armed forces your may qualify for continued education funding for your service to our country. The GI Bill has been a source for military veterans and active duty service men and women to obtain training and college degrees for many years. There are many sites and organizations throughout the US designed to assist you receive funding.
4. **Employer Reimbursement:** Many employers have employee reimbursement policies in place for continued education. Obtaining this funding will depend on your courses and if your academic goals match the organizational direction.
5. **Continued Educational Loans:** During this last economic downturn, there were several programs with financial institutes that offered low interest, high risk loans for professionals seeking educational funding. Some of the loans were based on co-signers credit worthiness. That took much of the pressure off the unemployed but allowed him/her the option to take some inexpensive accredited courses.
6. **Out of Pocket:** A more direct alternative would be paying out of pocket. This would require you to be really discipline and have patience. Adjust your Educational Map to compensate for the time to complete your education if you are paying out of pocket.

Sample of a Career Map with a successful Training Plan.

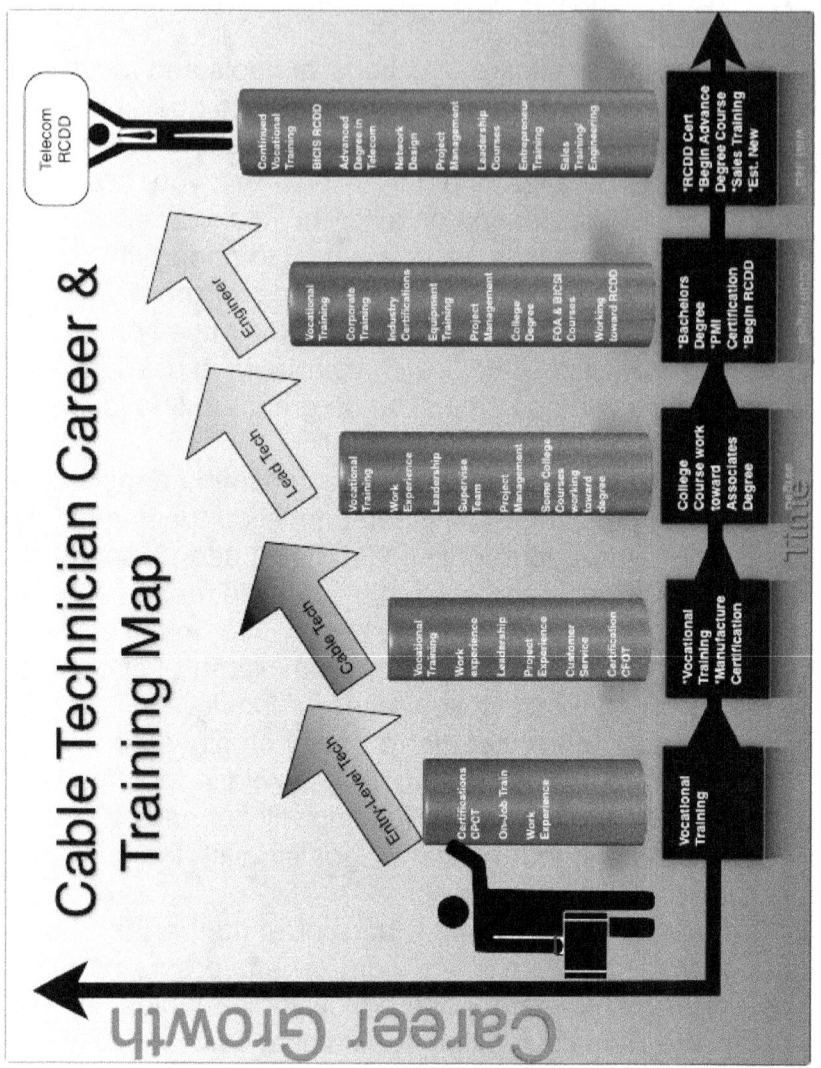

* Notice how each step of the career path is now paired with a training strategy.

* Each Career and Training Plan must have a progression. This professional will need a blend of educational services. Each plan will vary based on your ultimate career goal.

Career Mapping Sheet (Exercise)
Put your education to work

Lets begin to put the Career Map together. You will need a blank sheet of paper, pen and access to the internet. Write down the questions and fill in the blanks with your plan of attack. As you move along the questions, dive down to your professional goals and establish a training plan to match your career.

Question #1: What is the professional job title/position I am striving for? (End Goal)

Question #2: Currently, how close am I to obtaining this position? (Beginning Timeframe)

Question #3: Will I need to change jobs to obtain my goal?

Question #4: What is the job requirements of the End Goal position?

Question #5: Am I currently in the right market to obtain my goal?

Question #6: What are the educational requirements?

Question #7: Do I have a mentor who can walk me through my Career & Educational Map?

Question #8: How much money will I need to have to achieve my goals? Will I need student loans, credit , etc.?

Question #9: What colleges, vocational schools or training organizations offer courses that I need to advance my career?

Question #10: Will I have to work during the day and attend classes at night? Will this add more time to my End Goal deadline?

Question #11: Can I obtain accredited certificates to accelerate my career plan?

Question #12: Does my plan include leadership, supervisory roles, project management or OJT based milestones? If so, what is my plan to obtain that experience?

Question #13: Am I prepared to change jobs, cities, regions or even move out of country to obtain my goals? If so, what is my strategic plan?

By honestly answering those questions, you'll begin to fill in your Career and Training Map. Some people make this task complicated when it is not. The key to success is making your milestones obtainable. Below you will see how your Career Map begins to take shape after answering these simple questions. You will begin to add additional questions along with more planning. Over time, your Career Map will be a living action plan.

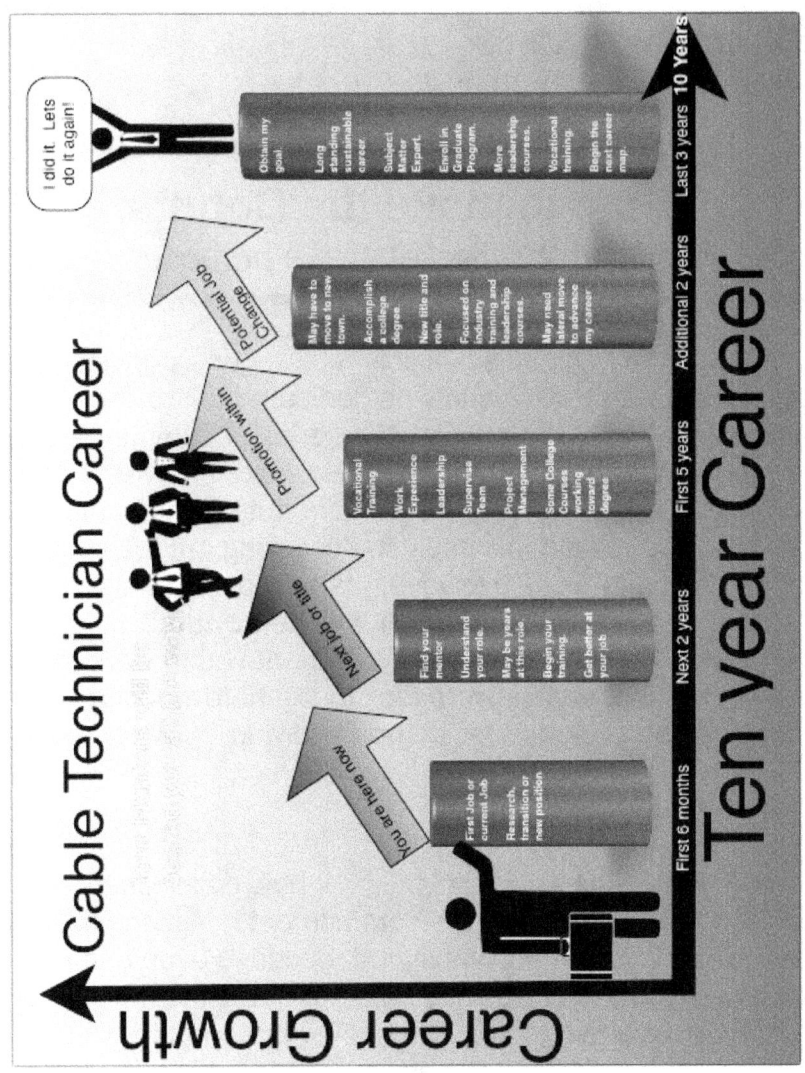

What happens if I obtain my End Goal early? Create a new task and begin again. The professional who becomes complacent in his/her career, eventually hits a wall in development and digress in growth. In simpler terms, "You will begin to loose sustainability in your profession".

Chapter 5

Time to make the Donuts.
Hitting the market with a purpose.

Back in the early 90's, I vividly remember a popular commercial with a chef who was dedicated to serving his customers. The company filmed a series of commercials but this one focused on the manager. He woke up every morning before dawn to make fresh donuts. One particular commercial depicted this cook sleepwalking out the door while heading to work. However, as he walked in his sleep, he continued to say, **"Time to make the donuts"**. I interpreted this philosophy as, "We'll beat you to work every day". It worked, and viewers took to the hard working attitude of the cook and his company brand.

Time to make the donuts

The goal of the ad wasn't to show how delicious their donuts were, but to show the commitment to serving the customers. Mission accomplished, because everyone knew that *Dunkin Donuts* was dedicated to doing the things that no one else wanted to do. The cook didn't want to get up that early, but he did out of passion to serve his customers. He had to beat his competition to the punch.

As professionals, we must have the same commitment to success as the Dunkin Donut advertisement. You may not want to get up and job hunt, but something within you must keep you on task.

That same passionate drive is inside of you. You should have discovered during your personal assessment (Compliance Wheel).

If your Passion doesn't align with your Purpose, Attitude and Spirit, you'll lay in bed and hit snooze when its time to make donuts. Your career should be a priority in your life. Identifying career opportunities and maintaining a sustainable path must be your focus. If not, your career goals will become derailed or someone will beat you to the deal.

I have learned from other top earners that working hard is easy to do, but being motivated beyond your best is what separates the successful from the pretenders.

All I want to do is golf and make money

In my early years, I visualized making tons of money and playing golf with the power players in business. That was my American Dream. As I began to earn more income, my work load increased. I managed to find time for golf but my tee times were not the same. .

I was responsible for a huge part of our business revenues. Spare time was hard to find, but my career path was shaping out nicely. I loved my job and was certainly glad my career was developing according to plan. I accomplished my American Dream but not with the Hollywood spin. I ended up playing a lot of golf in those days but I found the top earners missing at the mid-day tee times. They were teeing off at 6:45 a.m. and finishing just in time to shower and get in the office to manage their fortunes. Not the American Dream with the Hollywood spin, but a great lesson about successful people. Golf was a hobby or luxury, but continuing to be successful was a primary focus.

What now?

Today, I think your personal desire to succeed will dictate how successful you will be in your career. That is one reason why I believe the advertisement had such an impact on me and other professionals. It showed how dedicated the company was to being successful in a highly competitive market. No different from the attitude current job seekers should have for their career development.

Finding Employment, receiving a promotion, or completing educational goals will be difficult to achieve. You will need motivation and drive to get you through the tough times. Just keep in mind that every morning you decide to hit the snooze button on your career, someone else is sleepwalking the hallway saying, "Time to make the donuts".

Don't become a Professional Job Seeker

Professional Job Seekers are individuals who spend a career in and out of jobs. They seem to be motivated by the search and not by sustained employment. Most of them are easy to identify after a few questions in the interview.

The experienced Professional Job Seeker may take longer to identify. I've seen it take up to thirty days before their true motivation begins to surface. As a Professional Recruiter, you always want to assist your client find the best talent available. Professional Job Seekers are tough to deal with once they are hired. You'll find entitlement attitudes, 9 to 5 workers and lack of team spirit amongst the ones who make it to the job. They're not motivated by career development and always looking at the green grass on the other side of the fence.

Are you motivated to get off the couch

Are you a Professional Job Seeker? What motivates you about your career? Are you driven by the success of a career or motivated by collecting checks? Motivation takes a lot of energy. Why waste it on negative action items? Be motivated to grow your career and get off the sidelines!

Here are just 5 simple questions that can help you stay motivated during your employment search. Remember, "YOU" are in charge of your career and without a balanced Compliance Wheel your daily tasks can be overwhelming.

Use these daily questions to hold yourself accountable while finding employment. Your motivation should be internal. Have a mentor hold you accountable if you need the additional motivation?

Question 1#: Did I maximize my career development efforts today?

Question 2#: What did I do today that could have advanced my career or obtain new employment?

Question 3#: How many phone calls did I make that could lead to my new job?

Question 4#: Why did I fail at job seeking today? What "MUST" I do tomorrow to keep from repeating the same mistake?

Question 5#: Who did I meet or speak to today that could increase my chances of finding employment or advance my career?

Why am I failing at employment searches?

Employment search failures are the result of a variety of justifiable reasons. Many of them are as simple as bad resumes, horrible communication, FEAR and the list can go on. If you look deep enough, you will find the number one reason you fail. "YOU".

You are the CEO of your own destiny, and the reason why you win or loose in life. Unsuccessful job seekers are those who don't take control of their career development. I would say that these are the workers who constantly look for a "hook up" instead of putting in some work.

There are thousands of qualified personnel in the workforce who don't understand that hand outs are part of an entitlement attitude.

For those who seek a hall pass for jobs, there is no such thing as a professional "hook up". Professionals like to assist other professionals who represent the relationship well. For instance, you wont refer someone who doesn't represent you in some form. I was told early in sales, "People buy from other people they like and trust". You can control your employability by building your brand. You must become someone who others can trust and feel comfortable with referring.

One of my colleague believes we all get lucky finding jobs from time to time. Maybe you can call it luck, but I believe professional luck is the byproduct of great relationships and personal brand. No matter how good you think you are, you will never maximize your potential if you can't sell other professionals your brand.

You are the CEO

Lets compare a Chief Executive Officer (CEO) with today's job seeker. The CEO ensures that the company is in position to obtain market share within the industry. He or she spends everyday looking to grow revenue and its increase the brand within the market.

The job seeker is looking to do the same thing. He or she is viewing every opportunity and positioning themselves for financial gains and career development. They both work hard on branding, presentations and building appropriate relationships that eventually become opportunities. Job seekers control the destiny of their careers just like the CEO drives the success of a company.

I have developed a job description to show how similar you are to the CEO of a major company. Personalize this job description to describe your role. Include additional duties that may not be listed. Post your CEO job description somewhere you can review it during your search. Hold yourself accountable as the CEO and don't take your job lightly.

CEO of Your Career
Job Description

General Responsibilities
- Responsible for the success of failure of your career
- Establish primary goals of the career
- Discuss the biggest issues facing your career
- Prioritize the major action items contributing toward your career success
- Identify and manage all the daily activities for your career.

Financial Responsibilities
- Manage the financial status of your career

- Budget your tasks and milestones
- Be realistic with cash flow throughout your career
- Evaluate all of your acquired assets and value your career accordingly

Risk & Liability Responsibilities
- Crises Management
- Determine which opportunities, relationships and roles are for the best of your career

Legal Responsibilities
- Ensure that the you are in compliance with the Compliance Wheel at all times.
- Review all contract agreements for your career
-

Marketing Responsibilities
- Analyze and manage your career as it is being marketed
- Evaluate how your career is being marketed and perceived
- Identify best methods to distribute your career throughout your target market
- Ensure your career can stay competitive with its peers
- Identify potential new products that can improve your career (training, college, OJT etc)
-

Personnel Responsibilities
- Update the family on all aspects of your career direction
- Evaluate the strength of your support team
- Evaluate and monitor your career organizational chart and infrastructure

As you can see, being responsible for your career is not the task of your supervisor. It's YOURS to own and manage. I promise you, once you complete this course you will view yourself and your responsibilities in a different light. Lead your career by taking ownership of it. Be your own boss and lead your career to success.

Procrastinators find themselves in last place

Are you a procrastinator? How do you know if you are a procrastinator? Well, typically you begin with putting things off until tomorrow that can accomplish today. Fact is, most people procrastinate. However, the good news is, it can be corrected. Job seekers can easily procrastinate their job search if they've been unemployed for an extended period. You find yourself making statements like, "I am going to wait until the economy turns around" or "I'm going to ride my benefits a bit before I find something else". These are excuses of why I can't be successful today. Active job seekers are not procrastinators. They are doers.

I am a procrastinator and I need help

One thing you can do to help yourself is simplify your tasks and get organized.

There is no set organizational tool to fix your procrastination. You have to try them all until you find the one that works for you. Don't beat yourself up if you find procrastination easier to deal with. Keep in mind that most people have to deal with procrastination at some point in their lives. Some are just better than others at overcoming the issues associated with it.

I've listed a few tips to help you break procrastination tendencies during your employment search. Creating a positive habit using these tips. They will boost your motivation and move you closer to your achieving your employment goals.

Beating the procrastination bug

a. Set daily tasks and prioritize them.
b. Carry a notebook or a pocket tablet to stay on task.
c. Stay away from distractions.

---

d. Include someone else to keep you honest.
e. Sweat the small stuff. It will set you free to tackle big stuff.
f. Stay positive and confident. Habits take time to make and break.
g. Break up complicated tasks in to phases or sections.
h. Keep a calendar that reminds you of things that have to be done today.

Tip: I teach my daughters a simple principle to live by. "Every action causes a reaction, but procrastination has no rewards".

How does this apply to my job search? Simple, you loose today because you didn't put in the work yesterday. For every day you loose the activity battle, it affects weeks ahead. That can translate in to falling further behind in your employment process and loosing momentum. Life is all about ups and down, forward and backwards. I firmly believe, you are either moving forward in momentum or loosing speed for your cause.

Chapter 6

Goal setting for the professional.
Winners set goals!

Goals are the easiest tasks to manage. They are short and long term tasks developed by you. Goals can be adjusted based on personal/professional circumstances. Goals can be defined as your plan or desired action in life or in business. You set them and only you can achieve them.

Planning session for your goals

Planning sessions can trigger a goal setting action item. The more often you conduct a planning session, the more you set and view your goals. You can create realistic goals once you identified clear objectives. Most people have defined goals or end results, but no clear strategy to achieve them. The most common are weight loss, promotions, economic achievements or over coming common addictions like smoking cigarettes. In any case, your planning session will determine those common goals for you. Once you can develop targeted tasks, categorize them as short or long term goals.

Over time, your planning sessions will begin to look more like strategic business reports. You'll have defined goals, line items, milestones and obtainable rewards to look forward to.

Short & Long Term Goals provide prioritization of your action items.

Your goals are prioritized in two groups; Short Term and Long Term. The actual timeline assigned to your goals decide whether they are considered short or long term. Most goals can be established in three year increments or over a ten year timeframe. Others may have short-term goals defined within days or over the duration of one month. Short-term goals don't have to be limited to days, weeks or months. They just need to be identified and clearly defined.

On the other hand, Long-term Goals are typically identified first and probably the easiest to build during your planning session. In most cases, the long-term goals are defined as the result and are accompanied by a long list of action items. While developing your long-term goals it is essential to list all the action items, manage the key milestones and then put them in to measurable short-term goal.

Goal management is the key to success

Are goals guaranteed if you identify them? No, but you manage your goals by developing necessary processes that assist with staying focused and motivated to succeed. All goals must be measurable through the outcomes. That's why you must make your goals obtainable. Plainly stated, "You're either going to meet your goals or you're not." I believe it is that simple and if they are not obtainable the goals are a waste of time.

When was the last time you wrote your goals down? How often did you review them? Goal planning and management consist of writing them down and reviewing them as often as necessary. No matter if your goals are realistic or not, remembering each of them can be a daunting task.

Many of my colleagues believe that you don't necessarily need to write them down, but I strongly believe its essential to success. Unwritten goals aren't accountable! Unaccountable goals are just dreams without substance. They have no written reference that they ever existed and are difficult to achieve.

If you are committed to successfully achieving your goals, you will be more than happy to record them. Once you document them, you should share them with someone who will keep you accountable.

Tip: Goal Management
- Allot time for a Planning Session for your Personal and Professional Life. This will determine your goals.
- Use your calendar and/or technology to keep yourself on task.
- Share your goals with a mentor or someone who will hold you accountable.
- Review your goals every few weeks or as often as necessary.
- Measure your goals to see if they are realistic.
- Reward yourself for achieving milestones within your goals.

My first experience documenting goals

Back in the 90's, I got my first corporate job fresh out of the U.S. Military. My first civilian boss would ask me questions about my goals each day. He happened to be a highly successful entrepreneur and CEO of several fortune 500 businesses. He expressed the importance of having goals and why you should keep them close by as reference. This was similar to my experience with military orders and commissioned assignment.

Over time, I noticed that he always wrote his goals down and focused on them often. Not an obsession. but a focus.

Once I decided to share my goals with him, I realized that he would hold me accountable to obtain them. Now my goal sheet became a living document with accountability measures. We kept each other motivated and our goals became a competitive game.

This was even better for me knowing that I had to obtain my goals to win the game. In the end, both of us were winners and our goals became a habit.

Below are some tips my boss gave me on goals and goal setting:

Tip:
- They should always, always, always be obtainable.
- Goals don't have to be overwhelming. You can have as many mini goals as you want. If you need three goal sheets, make them.
- Goals can be independent. You can have a personal goal sheet and a professional goal sheet. Just have a goal sheet.
- Don't let your goals sit on the shelf. If your goals are written and then put on the shelf, then they are just words on paper.
- Keep them close by.
- Read them as often as possible

Your personal playbook. Winning each day with goals.

One of my current business partners played ten years in the National Football League. He firmly believes that goals are the key to success.

Throughout all of the locker room and SuperBowl stories he told us, he'd always emphasizes having a personal playbook for success.

Mike believes that your personal playbook can positively or negatively affect your goal outcomes. He believes that your goals are a direct link to your success.

Without them, we have no direction, no purpose nor a plan to achieve them. What Mike was teaching me was to focus on the small stuff. Just like football, your career is a game of inches. You must fight for each one.

Most professionals leave out the details. I think that is why we hear the cliche, "the devil is in the details". My translation was to focus on your daily task sheet. Your daily task are the inches in the game of life you must fight for. If you begin to take on the little stuff each day, your losses will turn in to "wins". This is what my friend called his "Personal Playbook".

We all have the ability to "win" every day. The difference is some people play to win and others play to get by. Your daily, weekly or monthly "Playbook" is where you get your direction and instructions. In sports, you don't perform well when you don't know the plays. It's the same in business. You would fail if you don't know how to win each day.

Here are some examples of everyday goals during your employment search:

a. Win on the phones today by making 100 calls.
b. Be a Champion by getting one person to review your resume.
c. No breaks today. Lets get our work done in advance and take some time for the family this afternoon.
d. I want to have a potential employer answer my call today.
e. It is essential that we get 5 people to talk to me regarding my experience.

Others may be more specific

a. I must get in front of someone from AT&T at the networkers luncheon.
b. Bank of America is my targeted workplace and today I have the opportunity to meet with an Executive. I will show my value by getting 15 minutes to feature my knowledge.
c. This week I will sell $50,000 in retail items. Today I must have at least $10,000 to be successful in my weekly goal.

Do I have enough time in the day to accomplish all of these tasks? Many people I've mentored feel overwhelmed when I share the path to employment success. The truth is, there is no one answer and no magic wand. All you have is your **self accountability.** At the end of the day, it's YOU who is responsible for winning or losing. No matter the circumstances, if your goals are written well, obtainable and managed daily, you "WIN". Everyone likes to be a winner. Why can't you be one?

Goal Tracking and accountability for the Pro's

In 1992, I was introduced to the Franklin Planner management series. Believe it or not, it was while I was serving in the United States Army. It was the most nerve wrecking course I have ever taken. I felt overwhelmed at first. It was designed to teach our troops how to multitask after the first Gulf War. At the same time, I was learning how to get organized. I began to build daily, weekly and monthly goals.

I learned a permanent organizational skill that would help me become a stronger leader. My military days of the Franklin Planner System were all about holding yourself and others accountable. It also helped me accomplish more during the day as we (our Division) found many ways to eliminate wasteful time.

For example, each task given was written in a planner. The task was assigned a symbol of distinction and was managed during your work week. Once you were given an assignment, that task was placed in the managers planner. If it included other personnel, those resources were documented as well. Everyone was held accountable for completing the task and no one was allowed to slip through the cracks. The Commander would have daily update meetings and you would receive a hasty reprimand if you didn't have your planner present. Daily updates and accountability made our Division remarkably efficient over the first 6 months. The ROI had to be great because our troops got better. Most of all, I even found myself with more time to spend with the family.

Today's Franklin Planner Process

These days, you have iPhones, iPads, smartphone and laptops that remind you of daily tasks. It could be real hard to ignore a task if you have several different devices reminding you each hour. However, that is not the point. **The point is, sometimes the "system of accountability" is not there when you are the "only" one tracking your success.** There is no excuse with so much technology at your fingertips.

You can create your own processes

In 1999 I was tasked to take on a group of college graduates and coach them to a successful career in recruiting. This was a tough task but I quickly reverted back to my Franklin Planner training to provide them with some structure.

The first task was getting them used to accountability. This was rule number one. Furthermore, we had to find a methodology that kept us all on the same sheet of music.

This was substituted with our electronic calendar and a spiral notebook. This notebook was dated daily and kept on the desk at all times.

Over a few short months, these young professionals became comfortable sharing successes and failures of assigned tasks. Accountability was welcomed and our production increased. ***The return on the investment was $2.5 million dollars in revenue. Success began to follow them through a personal process, goal setting, task oriented focus and accountability.***

Tracking your goals are no different from tracking your tasks. You have to write them down, manage them during the day and develop plans and solutions for challenges. In most cases, we require that accountability colleague or mentor who will keep us on track. I use my business partners for professional goals and my wife and children for individual tasks. There is nothing like tracking your goals with an accountability partner.

No matter what works best for you, track your progress and measure your success. You can't learn to get better if you don't know why you are failing. Tracking measurement systems like planners, calendars, mentors and technology will assist you reach your goals and become an efficient job seeker.

This Goal Sheet will assist you:

1. Establish clear attainable goals
2. Have a plan of execution
3. Measure and manage your goals daily Have a timeline that is realistic
4. Clear and rational Action Items (This is your plan of action. Very critical to any task but changes the daily outcomes)

---

5. Include some potential challenges you foresee. (Be prepared for unexpected challenges) Have a plan of attack for those challenges and
6. Assign a Goal Buddy or Accountability Partner to your goals.

Goal Setting Worksheet

APSI	Completion Date for Goal _____

Goal Definition Section

My goal is?
_____
_____
_____

Why is this goal important to me?
_____
_____

Timeline/When do I want to complete my goal? _____
_____

What do I want to achieve? _____

Measurement Section

1. Goals left outstanding: _____
_____

2. Am I meeting my expectations? _____
_____

3. Where can I do a better job? _____
_____

4. What I am doing wrong: _____

Action Steps		Target date	Completed
1			
2			
3			
4			
5			
6			
7			
8			
9			
10			
11			

Potential Challenges	Potential Solutions	
1	1	
2	2	
3	3	
Goal Buddy #1	Goal Buddy #2	
Contact #	Contact #	

Alliant Personnel Solutions Inc.
5100 Reagan Drive, Suite 17
Charlotte, NC 28206
www.apsicorp.com

Sample: When developing your Goal Sheet, be creative but make sure you keep the essentials in tact. Your success depends upon a great goal sheet.

Additional Tips for tracking your goals:

Tip #1: Use the latest technology to help you. Calendars and notebooks can be kept on your cell phone or even on you laptop. Don't be afraid to learn and then use the vast amount of technology at your fingertips.

Tip #2: Make sure you update your goal sheet weekly. Some task are beyond a daily update and other tasks require support from team members.

Tip #3: Look at your goal sheet as often as necessary. Over my career, I have met many successful professionals who take this step extremely serious. Some carry them in their briefcase, others have a three ring binder, but many have them close by so that they can be reminded of what is important to them.

Tip #4: When managing your goals, you will not achieve every task as planned. Stay committed and focused on the long term goal. Remember to sweat the small items each day that contribute to the long term goal.

Tip #5: Don't give up! Don't give up! Don't give up! Remember not to give up! "Good things come to those who plan, execute, commit and are patient.

Chapter 7

Networking
The "Big Ugly" of job seeking

No employment strategy can begin without assessing your personal network. It's like asking yourself "what is my employment bandwidth"? Many scholars say that networking is the best way to gain employment. I can agree with that statement since I find over 78% of todays jobs hidden to the public. Some organizations make a priority to provide financial rewards for referring new skilled employees. Their philosophy is to have talented employees refer other talented employees. Meaning, professionals will be looking for other professionals within their network. The old cliche' states, "It's not what you know but who you know that can get you the job".

Networking is calculated and should be measured in all job searches. Its all about making the right connection with the right person. Building your personal network will ultimately improve your professional bandwidth. You have to focus on improving your network through online resources, activities, meetings and social functions. To attain success in developing your network, you may be required to go beyond your capacity and outside the comfort zone.

Build your relationships for sustainability

Job seekers have to work extremely hard on building relationships. You have to create them and then maintain them over the course of your career.

Be clear in your initial intention but make sure your new relationships feel comfortable pointing you in the right direction.

To master the art of building relationship, you will need to practice. Focus on making new contacts and strengthening old ones. Don't be surprised if you are having coffee with the director of a growing business after 60 days of consistent networking. Making the right connections will yield great returns. Strong relationships are the gateway to sustainable networks.

Networking is a perpetual activity. It takes some time to get going and can easily die down if you do not cultivate those relationships. Think of it as an investment. Your ROI in networking will depend on how much you put in to it.

Be the "Opportunist". It's the BIG UGLY of networking.

Some people have an uncanny ability to be at the right place at the right time. It seems to be a skill they're born with instead of a learned trait. I used to wonder how they would strategically placed themselves at the moment of reward? It took many years for me to figure out that those very lucky individuals were not as lucky as they wanted me to believe. *They were quite brilliant in their planning, more importantly, calculated in their approach*.

In this chapter, I am going to share with you how to be strategically lucky. I will provide you with tips and guidelines that will position you for success. Executing the strategy correctly will let some of Lady Luck to rub off on you. I want to warn you of the sacrifice it will require. Nothing good comes without a price, and this strategy requires you to exchange the fame and glory for the unpopular practice of a daily grind. Some of my colleagues have defined this process as the **"BIG UGLY"**. How to get good at the "Big ugly" task? Networking!

Let's Network

Go back to your teenage years and reflect on your social outlets. I am sure you will find yourself trying to fit in with the popular crowd or planning to get in front of your High School Crush. You were acutely strategic in how you made your way to the lunch counter where he or she "just so happen" to be seated. You became quite the opportunist, and every chance you got, you schemed up a plan on how you will get in front of them. Once the opportunity presented itself, you already had a script of what to say. You mustered up the strength and then said, "Are you free this Friday night?"

Did your plan work all the time? Probably not, but did it allow you the opportunity to have a chance? Yes! You have to be in front of them to ask them out to the dance.

You can't win the lottery if you don't buy a ticket! Stop waiting for the ticket to fall out of the sky. My dad told me once, "he's never seen a lottery winner who didn't buy a ticket." His point is relevant in your job search. I never seen a person get hired who wasn't looking for a job.

Throughout my career, I have seen examples of powerful professionals who where great opportunist in the business world. **These were individuals who just happened to be at the right place at the right time**, **but this was happening all the time**. In Washington, DC we would call these individuals Power Players. I befriended one of the Power Players and became a student of the game. He taught me some key lessons to becoming a "Player" within my market. These same principles can be translated to job seekers. I have provided a few of them for you below:

* You must have a target market.
* Never lose sight of your end goal.
* Get over the nervousness.

* Be confident in who you are and what you bring to the table.
* Do your homework? Know who you are talking to and how they can help you.
* Learn to avoid conversations that lead to bad outcomes but develop the skill of conversational direction. (leading your audience to your goals)
* Create a personal buzz. Don't be afraid to be the subject of conversation. It can create a positive buzz.
* Always, always be professional. Don't do anything foolish to destroy all of your hard work.

Within twelve months of working these principles, we became known as regulars in influential circles and our businesses was being rewarded for all our hard work. I do mean hard work! It was UGLY, but the reward was well worth it.

I was learning some central lessons about positioning and how to make your presence known where it counts. I became a strategic opportunist. I learned this networking skills that I didn't think I had in me. I'm not as outgoing as some may believe, but it became fun over time. I learned to overcome my fear of massive crowds and public speaking in power forums. If I could overcome that fear, anyone can. It was the blocking and tackling part of the business. Everyone wants to be the quarterback but no one ever gives the offensive line credit for keeping him healthy.

People think networking is hard work filled with many "NO's" and "Not Now". It can be embarrassing at times but, the rewards are greater than you can imagine.

If you are committed to succeeding in your professional plans, you must become an "OPPORTUNIST". Learn to network with powerful people.

Expand your bandwidth of influencers and begin your career with a little more luck on your side.

Time to get ugly. Your Strategic Target List

Lets start with understanding "WHO" you are targeting. You must establish a client list of organizations that match your professional profile and career path. Sales Executives are taught to develop a list of clients that maximize their efforts in growing business. Finding employment is the same process. The only difference is you're looking for jobs and the sales executive is selling a product. Everything else is the same. In other words, your tasks, work ethic and presentation is the same.

How do I develop my target list? Start by asking yourself prospect qualifying questions like:

Qualifying Questions:

*What organizations within my commuting radius hire my skill set?
*Does this company use my skill set?
*How many employees within the company have my background?
*How accessible are is the decision makers?
*What other organizations hire for my skill sets?
*Do I know any "persons of authority" in these companies?
*Do I know what the hiring process is, challenges, or extended hiring cycles that will prolong my entrance?
*Does my contact (someone you know inside) have the ability to endorse me?
*Does the company hire through recruiters or outsource firms?

**These are just some basic questions to help you develop your plan. Remember, your strategic target list is vital to beginning your networking process.

It is better to know exactly who you are looking for vs. looking for anyone to help you in your search.

Once you identify the companies, POC's and have your endorsement, it's time to hit the networking scene.

Social Media, networking and your next job

In 2011 over 20 million unemployed professionals found their current job using social media forums. These are individuals who have embraced the social networking era and used forums such as Facebook, Twitter and LinkedIn as a source to connect with hiring managers throughout the United States. Many surveys conducted with individuals who are seeking employment suggested that successful prospects had a profile presence on at least two social sites.

Interesting facts about Social Media Sites:

* There are over 145M active Facebook users (*Ogilvy & Buddy Media*)
* By 2012, 1 billion people are projected to have a Facebook account (*Time magazine 12/7-1/3 edition*)
* Over 45% of Internet users worldwide interact with social media (*TNS global)*
* More than 37% of US small & micro business would use social media more if they had more time (*Vistaprint*)
* 46% of micro business owners use social media (*Vistaprint*)
* 17% of US online consumers have a Twitter account (*ExactTarget*)
* YouTube reports over 450 million unique users visit the site each day (*jeffbullas.com*)
* Google+ is reporting over 24 million users in 2011 (*jefbullas.com*)
* Google+ was the fastest social network to reach 10 million users at 16 days (*jeffbullas.com*)

---

* LinkedIn has close to 120 million user/members
  (*digitalbuzzblog*)
* As of August 2011 LinkedIn is reported to operate one of
  the worlds largest professional networks
  (*linkedintobusiness.com*)

These surveys are showing that job seekers are becoming more technically competent with computers and mobile technology. Professionals are using them to communicate on a global scale searching for hidden jobs through their network. It shows that users of these social networks are doing more than just keeping up to date with old acquaintances. These are users who are communicating with the world through blogs, social sites and corporate accounts. If you are not connected now, you may want to rethink your employment strategy to include the largest networking forum in the world.

How can these sites help my network?

Over the last 5 years, more than 90 percent of US businesses use social media as a recruiting source. Furthermore, social media also serves as an evaluation tool for the employers. Social media sites are serving as a positive source for communication. It's a virtual open source of your social habits, clientele and activities you engage outside of the professional venues.

Social media sites can provide a global view of opportunities within organizations that you would have little access to in traditional networking forums. These are called "Hidden Jobs Markets". Hidden jobs represent over 75% of the job market today. These are opportunities that are not advertised to the public. You would be correct to assume they are the most difficult to acquire if you don't have a solid network.

Part of having a successful social media employment campaign is focusing on your profile. Your profile must cater toward your perspective employers. It should have language that matches areas of need within their organization. Your education and vocational certifications should scream "Hire me!". It takes time and an effective strategy for this employment tool to work properly. Focus on the profile, work your way down to the body of the profile and always include a photo.

Social Media Networking Strategy for employment

Developing a brand strategy for social media can be extremely overwhelming if you are not comfortable in the virtual communication world. Your profile can be viewed by all industry leaders, media, consumers and potential employers. A strong employment brand will depend upon your ability to influence stakeholders within social media outlets. Your next task is to create a strong brand through social media. Make your profile scream professional. Allow it to work for you while you are sleeping. Below are some tips to help along the way:

* Create a buzz for your profile.
* Participate in conversations and chat rooms.
* Position yourself as someone of interest in your industry.
* Promote your expertise and experiences.
* Engage in industry groups and begin to socialize with your peers and potential supervisors.
* Get as many people engaged in your post. Meaning get people talking about you! Its O.K. to be noticed and be noticed as someone of interest.
* Send connection request to hiring managers who may be interested in your background.

Creating a buzz in your social media outlet, you will find yourself in social circles that lead toward employment. How is your social media game these days?

How would you define your social media status? Are you a power user, social butterfly, every now and then or non user? Take some time over the next few days to create your social media strategy. Begin with your personal profile on at least 3 of the major sites. Explore the user groups and then begin making the right connections.

Here are a few of my favorite social media sites:

Facebook/Myspace
Facebook and Myspace are excellent forums for connecting with school, family and military friends but not the best professional forum if you are not careful with how your page is managed. Focus on reaching out to other professionals and separate personal and professional fan pages. Also, use a tasteful photo as your avatar. You don't want to have your spring break photo as your avatar while searching for employment. Keep in mind that employers are now using Facebook as a background reference for the character of new employees. So, be careful.

Google+
Google+ has the potential to be a more rounded forum for social and professional activity. It is almost like having Facebook and LinkedIn all in one. It is gmail driven so you will have to create a google mail account but, that is a free service. In google+ the key function is the ability to separate your personal and professional circles. The application is user friendly and is one of the fastest growing social media sites in the world.

LinkedIn
My personal favorite social media site. This is the place you learn how connected you are and how other professionals view you. At the LinkedIn site, this network is built on layers of connectivity. You can request a "warm" introduction through mutual friends to someone who may be able to progress your career. You are also allowed to join up to 45 social groups where you will find thousands of professionals who are interested in the same industry areas as you are. It is a powerful tool and one I highly recommend to all professionals.

Twitter
This is a social media site that will allow you to connect with people you don't know based on your interest. You can follow just about anyone who has an account and anyone can follow you. Followers must find you interesting so tweet strategically. Again, your profile will be the first place interested followers will look at before they select to follow you. If you can generate enough interest, Twitter can be highly effective.

YouTube
Using video as a social media marketing strategy can be highly successful in today's virtual video focused market. It is one of the fastest brand distribution mechanisms on the web. Outside of a few minor challenges getting your videos online, the opportunity lends itself for you to promote your brand through video networking. Once you have established your videos, you can market them on your Facebook, Twitter Account and Google+.

Pros and Cons of Social Media
Pros:
* You can use social media to inform your target market of your employment goals.
* You can build your professional brand.

* Improve your technology knowledge.
* Learn more about other skills, products and professionals.
* Cost effective.
* You can establish a mass marketing campaign to get the word out on your professional intentions and target companies.

Cons:
* Time consuming.
* Access to your personal network.
* Everything you publish is open for the world to review and critique.
* Doesn't help you build your face to face communications skills.
* Tough to know who is authentic and who is not.

Put your Network to work

The term networking is tossed around the professional workplace more loosely than any other term. Many of us are taught to network but never told how to effectively execute. We assume that business professionals know how to target the right people. WRONG! It is totally the opposite. Most professionals don't know how to target the right contacts. This is why you must practice, practice and practice some more.

Chapter 8

Using technology to find jobs
SEO for employment

Every hour, millions of internet users use some form of search engine to research information. It is reported that over 16 billion searches come from the U.S. alone. Just 15 years ago there wasn't many options for search engines available nor was there a valuable information listed to research.

Today we have Search Engine Optimization (SEO), which is a marketing process that will position your product or organization on the internet to be discovered. In the same matter of positioning your company through SEO, I've discovered a way to position your personal brand to economic buyers using the same SEO principle. The process is a simple equation:

(Candidate + Decision Maker = Added Opportunities)

Although using search engines do not guarantee employment opportunities, finding the right hiring manager will put you that much closer to your goal.

From my experience, I have found the internet to be the tool to identify and establish relationships with professional stakeholders within a target market. I utilized this tool for many years and it yielded millions of dollars in revenues not to include a vast network of client contacts.

The same formula and tools can be used to find employment opportunities as well.

For the last four years, I have taught displaced professionals the SEO methodology and those who follow the instructions have found employment. Here is what you need to be successful:

SEO for job seekers:

a. A well defined strategic employment plan
b. A target market of opportunities
c. Target organizations/managers
d. Defined Career
e. Professional contacts: email, phone number and social media profiles
f. Internet access with
g. Search engines (Safari, Yahoo, Google, Firefox, or Bing)

How does it work?

First you have to understand how search engines work. Search engines are tools that search throughout the world wide web looking for specific information you define. These engines have access to billions of webpages, replying to your request with information that fits your specific profile. In other words, you can type in what you want to search and the search engines look for it on the internet.

Searching for specific data

Boolean logic searches allow you to combine certain words and phrases to be placed in to a search box. When asked, your search engine will reply with the specific data you requested based on the word combination.
Some professionals take courses just to become more proficient with Boolean based search tactics.

In this short tutorial, our goal is to show you how you can use these tools for career development. This boolean method can connect the **Candidate** to the **Hiring Manager** to yield the **Opportunity** just as our formula depicted above **(Candidate+Manager=Opportunity)**.

Boolean searches use operators or key words that assist with narrowing your search down to specific results. Success if based on using operators such as: **Or, Not, Near** or even Quotation Marks **" "**. You can use other operators but these are the most popular. A key tip is consistently increasing your request data using the operators and breaking down your search for increased accuracy. There is no limit to operators you can have in one search.

Lets try a quick exercise. Go to your selected search engine such as Google or Bing. Type in a set of search terms using Boolean operators and begin to work your search results. I have included a sample of a typical Boolean search tool outline for you to use as a guide as you begin to practice on your own:

Microsoft AND Telecommunications AND Manager AND Jobs AND 704 AND Charlotte AND email address AND NOT Technician.

What did I ask the search for?: I'm looking for all the Telecommunications Managers Jobs at Microsoft in the area code of 704 in Charlotte, NC. I don't want the Technicians. Below is what you would begin your search in the search engine. I didn't want Technicians because I am a Sr. Manager who is looking for mid-level positions only.

The Boolean search interprets your search request in the following format:

"This job seeker would like for the internet to gather all links to websites that include the word **Telecommunications,** as well as the word **Microsoft,** as well as the number **704,** and the word **Charlotte,** and the word **email address**, but they don't want me to include sites that have the word **Technician**".

The beauty of this search tactic is that you will be overwhelmed with search results. Every website within your requested information will turn up. This includes access to information on hiring managers, email addresses phone numbers within the 704 area code and every job posted. This is amazingly accurate information for you to use and all you have to do is GET TO WORK.

One thing to keep in mind, without a clear defined strategic employment plan, you will find this methodology overwhelmingly difficult to manage. Understand, the key is managing the information you receive. You need to have a plan in place, then you connect to future business contacts. These contacts you turn up can reveal hidden jobs if you know how to ask properly.

What will you find during your search?

* You will find contact names and numbers of stakeholders.
* You will find names and contact information of individuals who can move your initiatives forward.
* You will learn your target company focus and hiring markets.
* You will find LinkedIn profiles of key contacts.
* "Hidden" jobs that are not typically advertised.
* News and Press Releases.
* Contract awards and projects.
* And much more...

To master the Boolean search tactic it will take some time and practice using other search engines.

The more you play with Boolean search engines the more you learn about your industry, market and its opportunities. As you become more proficient, you will find it easier to uncover non published job opportunities. You will begin to leapfrog your competition and know exactly where you are going in your own professional development.

Chapter 9

Develop a winning sales script
Learn to do what the actors do

The hardest thing to get over when learning to sell yourself or any product is the stage fright. I've never been an over confident person, so presentations was my worst nightmare. Fear of failure would creep in and I would become uncomfortable not being in control of the outcome. No one wants to fail, and having a simple conversation go wrong can ruin the entire day if you allow it.

In the early 90's I met a gentleman who moved to the East Coast from California. He was an inspiring actor, and scripts were a normal part of his life. He taught me that anyone can learn a script and incorporate your own personality so it doesn't sound artificial. I took his advice and began to implement scripts to my daily phone conversations. The scripts then migrated toward my networking events and ended up in the board room where I began to close deals.

Scripts don't have to make you feel sleazy or shady. They can provide you with a since of confidence and eventually make you a stronger communicator. Today, professionals place a premium on being able to communicate clearly. Scripting a conversation can be the beginning of a relationship that ends as a new opportunity. You just have to focus on a script that places an emphasis on continued dialogue. This gets the conversation going and keeps it moving.

Desired outcomes of your first script

When developing your first script, you should always have desired conversational outcomes. Use your search engine tools to research your contact. This gives you a better understanding of your target prospect and about their environment to uncover the hidden jobs. Using the knowledge uncovered in the SEO exercise, direct the conversation to your outcomes. During your conversation, look for buying signs or "easy yes" statements, verses a "hard no" during the scripted conversation.

Tie-in questions can be very effective while directing the conversation. These are questions that connect your skill or expertise to the needs or interest of the script recipient. Tie-in's are conversational drivers that extend the conversation and help you stay on the script agenda. Too many professionals spend time conversing with a prospective client and then leave the conversation achieving none of the desired outcomes. It is important to develop your script with basic outcomes in mind.

Your desired outcomes could range from:
* Getting a better understanding of the products the prospect business group uses.
* Gaining trust through your professionalism.

* Get the recipient to relate to your professional goals.
* Receive referrals.
* Have the prospect volunteer to invite you to an event, meeting or interview.
* Build professional trust.

Sample Introduction script:

Having a basic template is a great starting place to build a professional script. Direct your conversation and be clear in your intentions. Build upon this sample and incorporate your personality so that it flows with who you are. Remember, you are selling yourself, therefore "you" are the product. What you say and how you say it can affect your outcomes.

Opening Statement

YOU: Hi_____ (state prospects name)?

(Prospect: Yes.)

YOU: My name is _____. Do you have a quick minute? I am looking for some information on (Prospect Company Name)_____and I thought you may be able to assist me.

(Prospect: Sure. What you need?)

YOU: Great! (name)_____, I am a _____ who is certified in _____. I came across your contact information through (Referral, Social Media or Internet)_____.
I am in the process of deciding on a career move to your organization and I had a few questions regarding (prospect company name or division) _____.

(Prospect: Are you looking for a job?)

YOU: Yes, I am always open to new opportunities, but I have found success in speaking to decision makers within the prospect organization before seeking employment there. I want make sure my skills are a good fit first. Professionals like you understand the needs of the company, and I hoped that you could assist me.

YOU: With your permission, I was hoping to ask you a few questions to see if I would be a skill set fit at (Company Name)_____?

(Prospect: OK. I have a few minutes)

Sample questions YOU ask the prospect: (you must modify your questions based on the direction of the conversation)
1. What is your specific role at (Company Name) _____?
2. Does your business group hire professionals like me?
3. If not, what about other groups?
4. Does (Company Name)_____ hire (your skill sets here)_____?
5. Are you involved in the hiring process at all?
6. How often does your business group hire (your skill sets here) _____ or any similar skill sets?
7. Is there someone you can refer me to within the business group who manages the hiring process?
8. I understand (Company Name here)_____ was awarded a project recently does that project affect your business group?
9. Will (Company Name here)_____ need additional skills to fulfill the project obligations over the next 6 months?
10. Is there anyone I can speak to that can help me submit a resume for those future openings?
11. Does it make sense for someone with my background to pursue employment at (Company Name)_____?

The Close

YOU: Where do you suggest I go from here?

(Allow your prospect the ability to suggestion your next move)

The Double Close

YOU: I want to thank you for your time today. I know your time is very important to you and I hope that I didn't waste it.

YOU: I would like to send you a thank you card. What is a good address to send it to?

(Prospect: No, you don't have to do that)

YOU: Well (Prospects Name)_____, in these economic times you don't often find professionals willing to assist other professionals in their employment research. You have given me some great feedback and I just want to thank you for your time.

(Prospect: Ok, you can send it to 123 EX Lane, Cunnigham, NC 28173. Address it to me.)

YOU: Thank you again. Can I share with (Referral Name given earlier)_____ that you and I spoke and you provided me with their name?

(Prospect: Sure, thats ok)
YOU: Thanks again Mr./Mrs _____. Have a great day!

Do's and Don'ts of sales scripts

Do's

* Have a Strategic Goal
* Make sure you have researched that individual, business group or organization.
* Be clear and and use proper pronunciation.
* Try to smile when you talking to your prospect.
* Stand up and walk if it makes your feel more comfortable.
* Be humble in your approach.
* Ask for referrals to other professionals who can help you in your quest.
* Be prepared for "NO". In fact, expect it so that it doesn't come to you as a shocker.

Don'ts

* Don't Lie to get the conversation going.
* Be arrogant or aggressive to show confidence.
* Don't be long winded. Leave pause breaks for feedback.
* Be afraid of bad news. There is no such thing as bad news. There is just news.
* Don't ask basic information about the prospective company. You should have done your homework up front.
* Don't misrepresent your expertise. i.e. oversell your qualifications.
* Don't name drop someone who didn't give you permission or isn't in your network circle.
* Don't try to be someone you are not.

Chapter 10

Dialing for dollars
The Big Ugly has a little brother

What is Cold Calling?

Cold calling is contacting prospects over the phone or through other communication lines to promote oneself, product or service. Employment seekers use cold calling as part of the natural process to find employment in today's technical workforce. No longer can you use newspapers and circle advertisements to find you next job. At some point in your process you must find the opportunity and contact someone by way of phone or email.

Effective cold calling increases your employability by placing you in communication with someone who can directly have an impact on your career. The goal of job seekers cold calling is to:

- **Obtain information about the prospective employer.**
- **Obtain another contact who can push your initiative further.**
- **Get an open job description for your skill set.**
- **Talk to a hiring manager or decision maker.**
- **Get an interview which leads to employment!**

Cold calling techniques are a learned skill. Don't believe that you are born with cold calling expertise just because you have a specific personality. Some of the best cold callers I've ever managed were really shy and passive personalities.

They became skillful by practicing and scripting calls until it became natural.

They used a combination of research, emails and phone calls to create a client sense of urgency. These techniques can be used in the job seeking process as well. Lets put that process together for you.

Cold Calling Process

You must identify your target market. For the employment sector you want to know the following:

•Which companies look for your skill sets?
•Who can influence your hire within these companies?
•What job vacancies are listed on the internet?
•Contact emails, phone numbers and locations of individuals who may be interested in speaking to you.

Do your homework. Research thoroughly before you begin cold calling. You want to be able to share important information with your prospect employer. You'll appear diligent in your approach. Companies are impressed when you do your homework.

Some key areas to research are:
•Press Releases, Newspaper articles and Media coverage on the company.
•Contract awards.
•Major Projects the company is engaged in.
•News on new hires such as Presidents, CEO , etc. (There is always something to talk about when a company is clearly going in a new direction. This could be a great opportunity for your expertise to fit within the new executives vision)

Be prepared for questions about yourself and professional expertise. Be ready to use your script.

Don't get caught off guard when the client ask you some question about your intent. Stay alert and be ready for anything. Here are some tips for success:

Tips for success:

1. Have your resume readily available so that you can highlight your professional accomplishments.
2. Be prepared to discuss your education, training and skill level.
3. Don't use "UHM". Be clear in your responses.
4. Know your objective and don't be afraid to share them with your potential employer.
5. Lastly, be honest!
6. Have a plan prepared for the next steps. Be ready to schedule an interview, meeting or follow up. Tips for your action plan:
7. Have your calendar prepared during your cold calling process.
8. Be ready to schedule an appointment.
9. Don't push off the meeting! Get the appointment now; even if it is two months down the road. Put it on the schedule! (You can always reschedule but you can't always get that person back on the phone)
10. Have your email and contact information available.
11. Get there contact information. Email, direct phone line and address.

What is your communication level?

I spent ten years serving in the United States Military. Early in my career I wondered why all the Drill Instructors sound alike? I found my answer the first week of the Noncommissioned Officers School. The US Military leadership schools are designed to train leaders to manage large groups of soldiers. The major component of this special skill training is communication. Using your verbal abilities to lead men and women in and out of battle.

I was a country boy from North Carolina with a slight southern accent. My pronunciation was a bit off but no different from the soldiers from Boston or Texas. This is when I discovered that no matter the type of accent, Uncle Sam has a way of balancing out the communication barriers. We were quickly trained to direct a large group of soldiers with just your vocal commands. Any unclear instruction and you can be eliminated from leaderships school. You **HAD** to be clear in your instruction or you failed.

I passed the school and eventually established myself as a leader. I developed a professional accent and pronunciation became a number one priority for me. I got promoted and landed a prestigious assignment that required good communication skills. My job was to work with the high ranking officers on highly sensitive personnel issues. In that role, clear communication meant recognition and bad communication meant reassignment. After a ten year stint in the Armed Forces, I felt prepared for the professional world.

So why is that story so important? It's important to know that being clear and understandable is the benchmark for professionalism. I believe strongly that when interviewing, most employers have a tendency to lean toward the individual who can communicate vs the candidate with the most knowledge.

You must know your communication level during your job search. Spend some time evaluating your personal communication style. There are many online test you can participate in that will give you a great foundation to build upon. Once you understand your communication level, you can build toward being an effective communicator.

I have included some questions you can use when evaluating your communication levels:

Communication Evaluation Questions

•Do you run out of things to say when communicating with people you don't know?
•What is the educational level of your network?
•Are you consistently asked to add input in conversations?
•Are you a passive communicator?
•Are you aggressive when communicating?
•Do you dominate every conversation?
•Are you intimidated by people of wealth?
•How do you communicate with individuals who are extremely educated?
•How do you pronounce your words? (Good, bad or average)
•How is your grammar? (Good, bad or average)
•Do you feel you could use some communication training?

Tips: There are some great online tools that can assist you with identifying your communications level. These tools can further assist you with becoming a better communicator. Use your Boolean search to find a tool that suits your needs.

Communicating with good pronunciation

In today's business world, pronunciation is probably more important than your vocabulary, and in some cases your grammar. Job seekers must develop their overall communication skills. This includes speaking and writing, but many fail to concentrate on the word pronunciation.

Good pronunciation with a clear voice presents a higher level of communication quality. That transfers to the communication receiver as someone who is well educated, confident and informative.

For job seekers, it could be the difference between getting hired as a Technician or being considered as an Sr. Engineer. You could be well qualified but eliminated due to bad communication.

I spent most of my professional career interviewing candidates for clients to hire. I've seen too many quality candidates interview, but failed to communicate on the level of their resume. These are resumes that are professionally developed by someone other than the candidate. During the interview, the candidate fails to communicate and the resume seems falsified.

During my recruiting days, I often gave communications suggestions that some candidates viewed as arrogant input or rude. The purpose of my suggestions was to educate job seekers on the importance of professional communications. Those who took the advice showed professional maturity, but those who did not, continue to be professional job seekers. Take the time to evaluate your ability to communicate on all levels. Remember, managers love candidates who communicate well.

Good communication and today's job seeker?

Communications skill are essential to success in life. In most professional environments, people tend to spend over half (50%) of their day communicating in some manner. It could be speaking, writing or negotiating business deals. If you are spending half your day communicated at work, it increases as you get home. We are in the world of Facebook, Twitter and online chatting. Throw in modern day technology, mobile applications and you can easily increase the amount of your daily communication by 20%. Learn to properly communicate in and out of the workplace. Your professional communication doesn't stop once you clock out. Become well rounded and your employability brand will increase.

Call Reluctancy can kill your next job opportunity

Effective employment processes tend to begin and sometimes end with a phone call. This process sets a high premium on communication. Therefore, you must begin to get comfortable on the phone to be successful.

A dream job could be the very next phone call and your ability to promote yourself depends on it. So why are you afraid to pick up the phone?

Job seekers find making cold calls one of the most difficult task in the employment search process. Many of them find calling potential employers over the phone more difficult than speaking to them in person. Maybe it is a fear of communicating with someone they don't know, or it could be a fear of promoting themselves to strangers. In many cases, it paralyzes the career.

I am positive there are hundreds of scientific reasons for call reluctancy, but experience has shown me that it's the number one culprit of failed success for professionals. Call Reluctance is not bias to just entry level professionals. It affects experts as well. Call Reluctancy is an emotional state that diverts your focus from your actual task. It can be a simple form of procrastination that delays your success. In worst cases, it can be an anxiety that takes your drive away from making that important phone call.

Call Reluctancy can also affect your telephonic interviews. This happens when you allow your fears of speaking to new people block your ability to shine. In other words, your call reluctance can stall your employment progress if you don't break away from its grasp.

Examples of what can cause Call Reluctancy

1. Fear of Rejection. The word "NO" is powerful and holds a fear factor that can stop your progress and professional development.
2. Naysayers and negative support groups. Negative supporters can spawn a fearful attitude and create stage fright.
3. Fear of using the telephone to communicate.
4. Over Analyzing action steps. (Individuals who spend too much time over thinking simple tasks)
5. Thinking you are inferior to the prospect.
6. Trying to be too polite to the prospect. (Don't want to intrude on someone else space)

***Now the question is, do you have a case of call reluctance?**

Here are some typical examples of the causes listed above. See if they describe you and then focus on a solution to help you break the call reluctancy bug.

Sample #1: Fear of Rejection
This is the individual who has a very large ego or low self esteem. Don't want to hear the word "NO" so they avoid being put in situations where being told "NO" can happen.

Solution: Train your self to expect "NO" but be prepared for the yes. Practice makes perfect for this person. The more cold calls you make, the more comfortable you become with rejection. A good exercise is to pair up with a peer and attend network functions or public events. Set a goal of getting business cards or information. The winner of the contest gets a reward. This training tip can help eliminate your anxieties of being rejected.

Sample #2: Fear of using the telephone

This is the individual who is terrified of using the telephone to engage with strangers. This person gets tongue tied, flustered and even break in to physical hives when asked to call someone they don't know.

Solution: Develop a script and practice objections until you are prepared for every scenario. As a Sales Manager, I developed a two minute drill training session for my young sales staff. Just like the name of the training process, it is based on thinking quick on your feet and answering difficult questions at the same time. Once my staff had memorized their individual scripts, the two minute drill became easy. Phone call activity went up and revenues soared. You can use a peer, friend or family member to help you with this drill. Highly effective and helpful.

Sample #3: Over analyzing the task

This is the professional who will ponder on the task alone. These are over thinkers and not doers. Individual who fall in this category spend more time researching, planning and developing plans that keep them from making the call. They only leave a small window to complete the task which eliminates room for failure. That eliminates time for success.

Solution: Get organized. Carve out specific time in the day to make your phone calls. Stick to your schedule and don't allow anyone or anything distract you from your duty. Go to a quiet room or lock your office door to get away from outside distractions. Do your research on the prospect but don't let it consume your time? Get to the phone as soon as you can.

Sample #4: Fear of being inferior

Some professionals disqualify themselves for their lack of skills. They feel as if they don't have something critical to communicate with affluent or powerful people.

This is the sweet spot for finding employment because you must convince the executives that you are the best candidate.

Solution: Join professional user groups where executives may participate. Spend some time chatting with them and getting comfortable communicating with individuals of influence. Another suggestion is to befriend a high ranking executive as your mentor.
He or she can break down your fears by using warm introductions to their colleagues. One other tip is to attend more networking functions.

Sample #5: Trying to be too polite
This is the person who is absolutely too polite. They feel that asking questions is intrusive or rude. They want everyone to be harmoniously in tune with each others initiatives without asking questions. They feel like those moment will present themselves. Polite call reluctant professionals don't want to invade other peoples space.

Solution: Understand your role and the responsibility of the prospective manager. Know that executives and managers expect to be approached by sales professionals and job seekers. That is part of the job. Some managers enjoy it and others do not, but you have to understand that most don't mind you asking good questions. Also, keep in mind that you are selling your employability brand. If you are too polite in your brand presentation, it could be misrepresented as a weakness.

These samples are just some of the areas in which you may be feeling some symptoms of call reluctancy. I've seen many professionals overcome them by just fighting the negative temptations to give up. You have to be patient in your employment search and making cold calls will take time, scripting and practice.

Develop your very own two minute drills for cold calling. Be hard on yourself or have someone else do it for you. You must be prepared for the worst.

Time to train

I use the military as a great example when training young executives. I share my military experiences to make a point of how to perfect your craft.

Military troops train 24 hours a day, 7 days a week for current or future wars. Some of the training is so intense that many soldiers don't make it through day one. There is a reason for the high intensity training. Military leaders are paid for one thing. Lead troops successfully in to battle and bring them home safely. To accomplish that enormous feat, you must train like you fight. Soldiers are specimens of perfection!

With this perfection methodology, many combat soldiers are mentally prepared for battle and rarely surprised in combat. If job seekers had the same philosophies, unemployment would be a lot lower. It's no different from overcoming your own fears and anxieties to be successful in the business world.

Similar to the military training, you must acknowledge your shortcomings, face your fears and train like your life depends upon it. Over time, making phone calls becomes natural and you'll experience a new level of success.

Chapter 11

Door to door hunting
Old school tactics that still work today

Are door to door searches really relevant in today's workforce? I say yes, and I can share my successes using door to door methods to gain corporate access. Up to the mid 2000s I used the age old technique to gain access to information on prospective clients. I learned this skill from an old mentor who was very successful in sales during the mid 80's. He knew I was a proud young executive who was afraid of rejection. He used this tactic to help me overcome my fear of rejection. It worked!

His tactic was simple, develop a strategic list of potential clients within the industry, have some scripted questions for each client, get in your car and go door knocking. It was that simple and it became fun after a few weeks of practice.

Today we use the term "beating the streets" as a definition of finding employment or business development. Many naysayers will tell you that door to door employment searches are not effective. I've personally seen them work incredibly well. For instance, I taught this format to a group of young adults who attended one of my training programs. One of the graduates took my door to door tips and found employment within several weeks. He literally walked on a project site (which he strategically planned) and introduced himself to a Project Manager. This manager just happened to be desperately seeking help. How convenient was his timing?

That chance encounter (wink, wink) turned in to a first class referral to Personnel for an interview, background check and sustainable work.

There is an art to door to door employment searches. Your strategy "MUST" match our background, skill level and industry. Meaning you don't want to try the project walk approach if you are a Professional Engineer. Your tactic may be to visit the corporate office within your region and pay a quick visit to gather some information.

I know it sounds crazy for today's job seeker, but it can work to your benefit. Despite knowing there is a higher rejection rate in this process, you can position yourself as the ultimate opportunist if you can get by the "No's". There is nothing like being at the right place at the right time. It has happened to me more times than I can share. Besides, what better way to collect real time job leads than spending time with a project supervisor? The information you gain can be the difference of getting employed immediately, or never being considered.

Be deliberate and don't wast your time

Don't waste time targeting a prospect if there is a hiring freeze? What do you mean by hiring freeze? How do I know that? You can't get that type of information from the internet. That's information you obtain only by speaking to someone within or close to the company. This is the business intelligence you need to develop a successful employment plan. Do you want to target XYZ Corp for several weeks only to find out that they are going through a hiring freeze? No you don't. You can't go back and reclaim those lost efforts. You can only move on, but next time have a better plan.

How to effectively conduct door to door employment searches?

1. Research your prospect. (Make sure they hire your expertise)
2. Develop a travel radius with your prospect clients within it.
3. Have reliable transportation.
4. Don't park you car in front of your prospects business. (Park close by and spend time preparing for your introduction speech)
5. Have your newspaper clippings, press releases and news worthy information memorized for each walk in. (You are on a "fact finding mission" to see if there are employment opportunities only. You would like to know who to contact and when will they be available?)
6. Dress for the client you are targeting. (If you are a technician, dress as you would be in uniform with the client. Let them see you as you would be in their environment)
7. Have a nonintrusive approach prepared. (Don't carry many job hunting items with you. Leave your resume in the car and carry only your business card)
8. Have personal business cards ready to hand out. (It is easier to exchange business cards than to give someone your resume. Worst case scenario, you will get a business card of someone you can follow up with in the future)
9. Have your ID with you. (Some environments may require you to have an ID to gain access to the lobby. Be prepared.)
10. Have fresh breath and never smoke during door to door walk ins. (Gatekeepers hate the smell of fresh smoke as you walk through the door. Save your cigarette as the reward for your hard work)
11. Expect "NO" but be prepared for yes. (Don't let the "No's" discourage you. Play a game with yourself by betting on how many No's it takes to get a Yes. Winner buys the looser lunch!)

Door to door job hunting is very unconventional. Contrary to what you may believe, candidates are still finding employment going door to door. Door knocking or beating the streets may not work for the next CEO of a Fortune 500 company, but it could work for you.

Understanding the gatekeeper. Are they friend or foe?

A gatekeeper is a person selected to guard, protect and choose who and what passes through the doors or gates. Gatekeepers have been around for ages and have taken on a variety of identities and responsibilities along the way. From the days of guarding castles doors and running errands for dignitaries, to front desk receptionist and secretaries. Gatekeeper are a major part of business and here to stay.

Modern day business gatekeepers are very sophisticated and loyal to their job. They decide what information gets passed to the important people they serve. No one can get through without good reason and once your in, make it count. A gatekeepers level of authority go beyond protect and serve. He or she can make certain decisions that can determine if you are in or out of consideration. Mistreat a gatekeeper, and you'll never get through the front door again.

Gatekeeping is not for everyone, but the good ones are very valuable to the company. Hiring a good gatekeeper is like having your own Secret Service Agent and Delta Force Soldier wrapped in to one person. They are trained in identifying over aggressive salespeople and each has a direct line to public authorities, just in case someone wants to become violent. The influence level of a gatekeeper is where most outsiders fail to recognize.

I see them similar to an Army Infantry Soldier. You put them on the front line so you can manage the battle and fight force with force. Seriously! Gatekeepers are lethal and can disrupt your employment goals if you are not careful.

Getting past the gatekeeper

OK, here is a million dollar question. How do I get past the gatekeeper? Easy, just have someone connect you directly to the hiring manager. It is that simple.

I have tons of great gatekeeper success stories that I could write an entire series on. Most of them were pure luck (being opportunist), but the others were strategic. The strategic encounters are the ones that can be duplicated repeatedly. There is no guarantee that you can overcome the Gatekeeper, but you can get off to a great start if you understand them.

Gatekeeper roles

<u>**Gatekeepers normally are responsible for:**</u>
* Answering the phones.
* Keeping non employees out of company areas.
* Help and assist visitors. (Here you go! You are a visitor looking for some assistance.)
* Administrative duties. (Some do payroll, timecards, developing documents, etc.)
* Schedule appointments and manage executive calendars. (Here is a good one! They know when your prospect is in or not)
* They also conduct countless amounts of other critical duties that are connected to decision makers and stakeholders. (So be very careful of how you approach them. They can kill your employment opportunities for as long as they are employed there)

In over twenty plus years, I have found that getting past the Gatekeeper really comes down to luck, timing and your ability to communicate. What I do know about engaging the Gatekeeper is they control the lobby area.

If you are presenting yourself as a nuisance, in most cases the Gatekeeper will **NOT** assist you. If you come off as arrogant or a jerk, you **WILL** be escorted out by security.

Depending on the make up of your economic region, door to door employment searches may be easier than others. Early in my career, this methodology was a bit challenging. Try learning door to door sales in Washington D.C.? I believe I have heard "NO" in just about every language and format imaginable. I can recall walking in highly secured buildings not knowing where I was, and being told that I have a few seconds to exit the building. Talk about scary, I had to overcome my greatest fears, which made me a better sales executive and a more confident communicator.

Some job seekers may find themselves in a complicated workforce environment. Others may be in an open inviting market. I had to learn to identify secured buildings and to communicate with a variety of Gatekeepers to succeed. I strongly believe that every job seeker can be successful at the door to door tactics, if you develop a strategy and work your plan. Be patient, it'll take time. Learn to make it fun and expect to hear a "YES" every now and then.

To help you prepare for the door to door experience, I have provided you with some quick tips of how not to approach the Gatekeeper.

Gatekeeper Don'ts

* Don't lie when asked to be helped. (That is the cardinal sin of door to door walk ins. Stay honest)
* Don't just wonder in. Have a reason you stopped by. ("I came by because I read an article regarding your project award. I wanted to know the protocol of scheduling an appointment with Mr. Hiring Manager")
* Don't try to treat the Gatekeeper as if they are less than a valuable part of the organization.
* Don't use over aggressive body gestures to describe your passion and expertise. Be calm and professional.
* Don't wear too much perfume or cologne.
* Don't smell at all. If it is hot outside take time to cool off in between walk ins.
* Don't flirt with the Gatekeeper. No personal gestures or comments. Stay professional.

I'm sure there's a lot more information on the web, but my purpose of including the Gatekeeper is to educate those who may consider using the "beat the pavement" process to find their next job. All you have to do is develop a script, do your research and get out and enjoy the day. Someone once told me that, "Good things come to those who ask." Get out and ask someone about employment opportunities.

Chapter 12

Working with Recruiters
Gatekeepers of hidden jobs

No current job search is complete without at least one phone call from a Recruiter. If you have your resume online, chances are you will be contacted by a recruiter. Today it is common practice to go through a recruiting agency for sustainable employment opportunities. If your resume is well written and you have marketable skills, you will be found by a recruiter eager to put you to work. Will you be ready to deal with them?

Recruiting is not a new service

Recruiting services have been around a lot longer than most people think. It began in concentrated areas where professionals where hired to find specialized talent. Now, recruiting has grown to become one of the largest market segments in the workforce. In fact, many statistics show that the Staffing Industry will employ more talent than any other market segment over the next 10 to 15 years. Recruiters are no longer the black sheep of the personnel family. How do I know this? I have been in the personnel business over 20 years, and I have seen it grow to become a major employer in the global economy.

So, lets dive in to the world of recruiting and become more familiar with who they are, how they function and how they can assist you with finding your next job.

Who are Recruiters?

Recruiters are hired guns. They are men and women who are skilled at working with people. No matter how friendly you get with them, their loyalty is with the employer. I always told my staff, "You do not get paid by having a conversation with a candidate who is unemployable. You get paid by placing professionals who are employable." Always remember that recruiters get paid for placing professionals in openings and not to be your buddy. It is o.k. to build relationships, but in only works when candidates are marketable and the agent can place you.

Each industry has recruiters that specialize in specific skill searches. The industry will dictate how these recruiters engage with prospects. For instance, technology may have recruiters that focus on short term placements because of the project based work some engineers perform. Another scenario would be legal firms. Recruiters who are within this field may spend more time focusing on longer term direct placements. That is due to the security risk associated with personal documents. Your individual recruiting process will depend on skill set and target market.

There are many variations of recruiters and recruitment services, and job seekers must know how they can positively or negatively affect your career.

Types of Recruiters

In the recruiting world we break our expertise down in to a few categories:

* Temporary Agency Recruiter
* Head Hunter or Executive Service Recruiter
* Human Resource Generalist
* Retained Recruiter
* Consulting Firm

Types of Recruiters Explained

Temporary Recruiters: Are recruiting agents who focus on fulfilling job orders assigned by their client. These are high transactional search agencies that have short and long term opportunities for you to review. The recruiters are highly aggressive and could be the access you need for hidden jobs not published on the traditional job boards. Temporary Agencies are the most popular and diverse in the business. Some often have a Direct Placement Division but will have a wide range of needs to qualify for. Therefore your odds of finding a position is great, if you find the right agency.

Head Hunter/Executive Search Recruiter: Head Hunters are usually considered the "white collar" recruiting specialist. The Head Hunters or Executive Recruiters work closely with stake holders, economic buyers and executive leadership to fill openings. You will find upper management and senior level opportunities with these agencies. The type of opportunities will range from temporary to direct placements. However, in my experience you will find more direct placements with these agents. If you fit within this area, you should expect longer hire cycles and tighter competition. Be prepared.

Human Resource Generalist: I added this group because they represent the mid-cap companies. Most mid sized organizations don't have the luxury of outsourcing the recruiting function, but they have internal human resources who are charged with filling the personnel needs. The majority of the HR openings will be direct hires, but the specialist assigned will use the same recruiting tactics to identify and employ the right talent. In the recent years, I find many HR personnel in corporate environments with recruiting experience from outside agencies. These are the good HR recruiters who have probably worked in a staffing environment in the past.

Don't under estimate the power of Personnel. They are the true gatekeepers of your corporate employment.

Retained Recruiters: Retained recruiters are the experts of their perspective profession. Their fees are paid upfront, and they have a deeper relationship with the economic buyers. Retained Recruiters may have an office within the client work site, and provide more personnel services outside of recruiting. I have found most retained agents to have expertise similar to the potential candidates they recruit for. For instance, retained recruiters in the legal field have been known to have some type of paralegal certificate or a Juris Doctorate. This provides the competitive advantage over other general recruiting agencies, therefore, justifying being paid upfront for the recruiting service. They are very specialized and well paid. If you are in a specialized industry, look for Retained Recruiters assigned to the target companies in your career plan. They don't have much competition, and the hiring cycle is a lot faster than traditional recruiting agencies.

Consulting Firms: These are the general experts of the bunch. Consulting Agency Recruiters are seeking talent based on needs associated with a turn key solution. Being recruited by a consultancy will normally land you in long term roles as a subcontractor on large projects. The recruiters in the consulting agency will have a strong HR or recruiting background, and function similarly to the temporary agency. The difference may be within the interviewing process. Many consulting agents own the solution, therefore they are your true employer. Some examples of major consulting firms would be companies like Bain, Deloitte, Lockheed Martin, Northrop Grumman, SAP, Computer Sciences, General Dynamics and EDS.

***Keep in mind. Every recruiting agency mentioned (outside of the HR group) has the power to hire and fire you. Many job seekers see recruiters as young college students who don't understand the real world. That is the wrong approach if you want to building the relationship.
These are young professionals who are taught to be very good at identifying areas in your background. They are the agent that will market you to a potential client. You need to work with them, educate them on you brand and build a real relationship with them.

Several years ago I read an article about power professionals in our workforce. The article mentioned the top 10 professionals you "MUST" have in your social network. Recruiters were in the top 5 along with occupations such as; Doctors, Lawyers, and Accountants. I would assume that today, Recruiters would be the number one professional with national unemployment rates hovering double digits. If you can find an agent who is a power player in your market, he or she will be the most valuable player in your playbook.

Here are some tips of how to identify the right recruiting agency that fit your employment needs.

Tips:

1. Your Recruiting Agent should have great relationships with the client. Ask specific questions about their client relationships. **Make sure the relationship is directly with the recruiting agent and not the recruiting agency.** You want a recruiter who personally builds great relationships.

2. Make sure that the recruiting agency specialize in your expertise. Good recruiters develop a specialized skill for employing talent in certain industries. Some are great in Information Technology other in Aerospace and Defense.

Stay away from recruiters that work on any open opportunity available. You are probably going to lose out to competition with specialized recruiting agents.

3. **Always choose the recruiter who is motivated.** Find the recruiter who is hungry for the placement. Remember, "Recruiters who are struggling are just Recruiters looking for their next career." Hook up with the "TOP" earners if you can. They can get you placed quickly.

4. Small shops may be the ticket. The bigger the firm, the harder it is to access the jobs. **Small firms have closer ties with the client.** They are more concentrated and place a higher value on the client's satisfaction. They also build better candidate relationships.

5. **Don't knock the home based recruiter.** He or she are independent agents who like working from home. There are thousands of successful agencies around the U.S. who are home based. Try working with the agent who comes from a successful organization. Be curious about their clients but give them a chance. They'll work harder if you are the "prize catch" to help them break an account.

6. Ask your recruiter to share his/her success. **You want to look for agents who have a track record of placements with the targeted clients on your list.** Successful recruiters are hard to find on the streets, but they are easy to spot in the office. You will know them when you see them. They'll be driving the nice car, wearing the nice suit enjoying the better side of life.

7. **Don't be afraid to interview the recruiter.** Ask good questions. Be excited to know more about them but don't come off as a jerk. Recruiters don't get much credit from candidates they place. It is good when a potential candidate shows interest in the agent who will put them to work.

Look for: experience, expertise, client list and network contacts. This will give you a good snapshot of who you are dealing with.

8. **Keep in mind that long distance recruiting agencies have longer placement cycles.**
Placement will depend on their ability to sell your expertise from a distance. It can be done, but will take some time.

9. Try to find the Recruiting Agency who has the exclusive agreement with your target company. These organizations have access to all of the hidden jobs and can get you in the door. **Ask your agent if he or she has any exclusive partnerships in your industry?**

10. Ask the agent if they are certified. **Look for awards, certifications and distinctive accreditations.** Ask the agent if they're certified in recruiting. Look for particular company plaques on the wall or noteworthy recognition that showcase a relationship with a major employers. If they are not certified, don't be discouraged. There aren't many recruiting certifications in the market. It's important to identify the agents who are certified. Non certification doesn't keep them from placing you, it shows which organizations are serious about serving their clients.

Pro's and Con's of employment through recruiters

Pros:
* Quick turn around.
* Access to various jobs in your field.
* You have an agent doing the grunt work for you.
* Access to management contacts throughout the industry.
* Can keep you employed if you have the right skills.
* You gain industry experience through temporary assignments.
* Compensation is negotiable.

* Some salaries can be 15-20% higher for candidates who can negotiate.
* Opportunities to travel.
* Some present access to special clearances.
* Can serve in roles to gain entrepreneurial skills.

Con's:
* Lack of benefits.
* Short-term assignments / low sustainability.
* Project based work.
* Can be difficult to communicate your true expertise.
* Can be seasonal work.
* Can end at any time without notice.
* Harder to form client relationships.
* Recruiters can be loyal to the most marketable candidates.

Don't be fooled by the smile

Back in the late 90's, I had a very large client who hired my agency for recruiting services. My company was directly responsible for all the technical placements in the IT Support Group. This meant that everyone hired within the division had to be interviewed and employed by my staff.

I remember a candidate who was anti-staffing, and felt that he was above being a "temp". He was very talented and had all the necessary tools to fit within the culture of our project. Many of the team members thought he would be a great candidate for a lead position, since he possessed some management skills from a previous project. This made him an immediate prospect for the open job and future promotion.

There was only one problem with getting him hired. He did not know that I had a long standing relationship with the client, and many of the personnel in that department were "my" employees.

My company had offices on the premise with hiring managers and staff to ensure a quality deliverable. However, Mr. "I HATE RECRUITERS" managed to express his dislike of recruiting agencies before he had a chance to understand how the hiring process worked.

Throughout his interview process, he managed to upset the recruiters and was placed on the "DO NOT RETURN THE CALL" list by the client. Mr. "I HATE RECRUITERS", was not hired for the job even though he was the strongest candidate. If the gentleman had done his homework, he would have found critical information about the hiring process. Most importantly, he would have known who was responsible for the hiring. By bashing the recruiters about becoming a temporary employee, I am sure he will never be considered for employment by this client.

I praised my staff for their professionalism. The young recruiters serviced him professionally and with a smile. My staff knew that they control the opportunity. Mr. "I HATE RECRUITERS" had no clue that behind the young agent's smile, was a professional who understood the rules of engagement. They were the gatekeepers, and his unprofessional antics placed him further away from attaining employment. Many of the staff members had close friends who worked at other recruiting agencies. I am sure his name was placed on the "DONT WORK WITH" list throughout the region.

The Lesson Learned:

* If recruiting agencies are not your taste, stay away from bashing them.
* Recruiters and HR carry a lot of employment power.
* Always find out who is responsible for hiring. (Internal or External)
* Treat recruiters as professionals. Don't be fooled by their youth. Many are very competitive and professional.

* **Recruiters can black list you in your market**. Word travels fast when you act like a jerk.
* Recruiters are paid to identify, assess, evaluate and employ talented professionals. They are educated and trained to look for specifics in your background. At the same time, they are taught that potential candidates are the customer. Shouting at them probably wont get you hired.
* Don't be fooled by the smile. Recruiters are taught to be and remain professional during conflict resolution. You may think you are winning the battle but most of the time the recruiter will win the war. They have the power of employment!

Chapter 13

Interviews
How to kill the job interview

Become a professional job interviewer

Interviews are remarkably similar to evaluations conducted in the U.S. Military. When soldiers are up for a promotion or meritorious award, They are required to wear a formal uniform (military business suit) and present before a panel of leaders. This panel interview is called the Promotion Board or "The Board". One mistake during The Board interview, and it could cost the soldier money and opportunity. I learned a lot about being a professional preparing for "The Board" interviews. The lesson learned was very simple. Practice increases performance and perfection!

Fast forward several years, I was considered for a job and feeling very comfortable with my ability to ace the interview. Sitting in an office or in a boardroom was second nature to me. Why? I took what I learned presenting before "The Board" and applied it to my interviewing tasks as a civilian. It was a basic employment methodology using everything I learned as a soldier and dominating interviews with confidence.

Today, I teach job seekers tactics for perfecting employment tasks such as interviews and networking. Students have found success using them in academic settings, business environments, sales and non-profit organizations.

I've even used the same methods to teach my young daughters, who are excelling in both sports and academics. Some of the graduates have gone on to be successful entrepreneurs and business leaders. Others, such as my daughters, have grown to become scholastic athletes. So, what is the method? PRACTICE, PRACTICE, PRACTICE!

Are we talking about practice?

Practice makes perfect. Practice every essential task until it's perfected. Practice your basic communication capabilities, occupational specialties, formal speeches and in-formal meetings. Practice every task that can impact your career. The most successful people in the world practice their craft. Pastors practice, athletes practice, motivational speakers practice, elite military soldiers practice, teachers practice, musicians practice and even the President of the United States practice. If you practice your craft more often, you will see the fruits of the labor multiply over time. Keep in mind, only the lazy "wing it".

What am I selling in the interview?

Every client I have worked with has different styles of interviewing. Each hiring manager believes that their interviewing process is perfect for their environment. They are right, since the managers are not hiring for the competition. Their job is to effectively identify and employ the right candidate who can help the company increase productivity.

I had a candidate tell me that she was coached to view the interview process like hanging out with a professional family member. Wrong answer!

Your interview is your "SALES MEETING". Do not get coached in to taking the interview lightly! You are selling your employability brand. Don't lose site of that.

This is your chance to pitch your expertise. Don't blow it no matter how cool the manager may seem. Stay focused on why you are there and do not let your guard down.

Some managers are just as nervous as you are. They tend to need an ice breaker just as much as you do, so don't take it to be the opening to loosen your tie. Stay on task, and knock the interview out of the park.

Dress for the Board Room

Lime green business suit, neon yellow shirt, green neck tie and matching alligator shoes is how my candidate entered the building. I was taken a back when he met me at the front desk. "This can not be my candidate," I said to myself as I walked towards him. "Are you Scott," he asked? I wanted to say "NO", but I was taught to treat others as you want to be treated. "Yes", I replied, "but can we chat briefly. I have a problem to discuss with you"? I took that moment to explained why he would not be interviewing with my client that day.

My candidate did not understand the different dress code for business and personal environments. What is suitable for one culture, may not be acceptable for the corporate world. I gave him a brief list of appropriate attire for men, then spent an additional 20 minutes explaining what technical managers expect to see from technical candidates.

He was extremely appreciative of my assistance and asked if he could reschedule the interview. The blessing was, the job did not get filled right away, and he received a second chance to make an impression. My candidate interviewed well, received the offer and turned out to be an exceptional employee. What would have happened if he didn't get a second chance? How many interviews has he had and was turned down because of his attire?

How is your interview attire? Are you like my technician or are you focusing on improving your interview wardrobe? How you dress can say many things about who you are and where your priorities are. It doesn't make sense to buy the latest Coach handbag for $600.00, and not have a business suit. Upgrading your shoe collection doesn't substitute for not having your sleeves altered on your blazer. Be a pro, and look the part.

I have made a quick list of how your clothes can offer a hidden perception to managers before your official interview.

What your clothes say about "YOU":

* I'm not organized enough to even iron my shirt.
* My new $600.00 handbag and revealing club dress tells me you like to party every weekend.
* I am sloppy, and you can tell by the stains in my shirt.
* I am not the cleanest, and everyone knows it from the smell in my suit.
* I am looking for a new boyfriend, so this low cut shirt shows I am available.
* All I want to do is golf, so I don't wear a suit coat with my Nike polo, golf slacks and big belt buckle.
* I don't value my career enough to buy an interviewing suit, and you can tell because I borrowed my roommates clothes. By the way, my roommate is 4 inches taller than me.
* I am a chain smoker, and the smoke smell in my clothes remind you of a bar.
• I was nervous and just smoked one before this interview. (Also means that you will spend much of your time on smoke breaks)

Men's Interview guidelines

Two piece dark suit. Blue, Gray or Black are the best conservative colors. Other colors will only put more emphasis on the perfect combination. It is best to stay away from confusion if you don't understand how to coordinate the proper blend. Pinstripes can be tricky but solid colors are best.

Your shirt should be limited to a light colored blue or white long sleeve. Make sure it fits your neck correctly. Don't let it be too loose nor too tight. Have someone measure your neck for proper fitting. A well fitted shirt says a lot about you.

Undershirts are formal and professional. If you are a heavy sweater, wear a full shortsleeve undershirt. Heavy sweaters who wear sleeveless undershirts will perspire through the suite and that can be a distraction.

Socks have a combination formula. Dark Suit = Dark Socks. Light Suit = Light Socks. Socks should match your suit. If you are wearing a gray suit, wear dark gray socks.

Shoes are simple as well. Cordovan, Brown or Black. Wing tips, lace up or loafers work well for interviews.

Belt is black or brown. Your belt "MUST" match your shoes. No exception to the rule. (Black belt/black shoes)

Beards and Mustaches can be tricky. If you know that the company has a no face hair policy, you may want to consider shaving for the interview. Hair can always grow back. However, if you do have facial hair, trim it down. Don't allow the client to have a reason not to like you. Some long beard or goatees that are long can be a distraction. Trim those down.

Watches, necklaces and bracelets are allowed as long as they are not overwhelming.

CEO's are expected to interview in a Rolex, but the Service Manager may not understand why a technician is wearing one. Same goes for bracelets and necklaces. Anything that can be a distraction should be left at home. Tuck your watches under your shirt and keep necklaces inside your undershirt if possible.

Colognes should be used sparingly. You never know who can be affected by your brand of cologne. It could be positive or negative reaction. Don't take the risk. Refrain from wearing too much. I have met individuals who are allergic to perfumes and colognes. "DO NOT" spray the perfume on right before the interview to cover up cigarette smoke.

Women Interviewing guidelines

You first must ask yourself, "did I wear this at the club"? If so, you probably don't want to wear it to the interview. Now that is out of the way, we can talk about some basic guidelines for women during interviews.

Women suit attire is simple. Two piece matching color skirt or pants. Make sure that your suit is "NOT" form fit but business cut. Form fitting can be too much of a distraction if interviewing with a male manager. The length of the skirt should be long enough to cover your thighs when you sit down. Your suit pant length should not drag the walking surface. Have it fitted to a professional length so you don't risk tripping over it or causing a distraction.

Suit color is the exact standard as for the men. Buy dark blue, dark gray and black suits. Stay away from reds, pink and other colors that may be intimidating or flashy.

Shirts for women are a little more liberal than for men. Since women don't wear neckties, they wear a formal blouse that can be white, light blue, light gray, tan and other solid colors.

Do not wear shirts that can be loud in the interview. They are distractions.

Shoes are leather flats or heeled. (closed toed) The heels should be medium in length. Stay away from high heels that can pose a problem in walking up and down stairs or shoes that could be uncomfortable on a company tour. Make sure you are comfortable. Keep it conservative.

Hand bags should be simple. Don't bring a bag that needs its own chair in the conference room. Fashion is important but not why the company is hiring you. Keep it very manageable or something that can be carried without distraction.

Make up must be very conservative. Lipstick must be professional. Make a good decision with your cosmetics. Anything that can be ruined in rain or heat should not be applied.

Perfumes should be used sparingly. You never know who can be affected by your brand of perfume. It could be positive or negative reaction. Don't take the risk. Refrain from wearing too much. I have met individuals who are allergic to perfumes and colognes. "DO NOT" spray the perfume on right before the interview to cover up smoking.

**This exercise if to assist you conduct an inventory on your current business attire. Go through your closet and inventory your current wardrobe and begin to build a winning professional look that hiring managers love to see.

Basic Business Wardrobe Inventory Check List

Business Suit
Color(s)_____ _____ _____   Amount:_____

Business shirt / Blouse
Color(s)_____ _____ _____   Amount:_____

Belt(s)
Color(s)_____ _____   Amount:_____

Handbag(s)
Color(s)_____ _____   Amount:_____

Shoes(s)
Color(s)_____ _____ _____   Amount:_____

Underclothing
Color(s)_____ _____ _____   Amount:_____

```
┌─────────────────────────────────────────────────┐
│ Socks                                             │
│ Color(s)_____  ____  _____      Amount:_____ │
│                                                   │
│ Necktie                                           │
│ Color(s): ____  ____  ____  ____   Amount: _____ │
│                                                   │
└─────────────────────────────────────────────────┘
```

A little white lie can go a long way

Over exaggeration is the top eliminator of qualified interviewees. I believe most interviewees tell the truth about their education, experience and capabilities. There is another group that I have found to be flat out liars. Recruiters/Hiring Managers are trained to asked detailed questions to weed out the pretenders. In most cases, you can identify the pretending professional by their illusive responses to tough questions. The little white lie will grow in to a combination of lies. Before you know it, the interview is over, and you're known as the fraudulent candidate. Do not feel pressured to lie for the job. Managers asks tough questions to see how you respond, not what you respond with.

I had a client in the Defense Industry who fired a candidate for falsifying their qualifications. This Sr. Director was hired and working out well until Personnel conducted the annual employee audit. Most companies conduct audits to make sure all of the federal required documents are maintained for each employee. It is not uncommon to get a call from the corporate office asking for documentation that was missed in the on boarding process. In this scenario, the client expressed their right to press charges.

The Sr. Director was busted, and the client wanted to exposed the employee to the entire technology community. I am not sure what the terminated employee lied about, but it was serious enough to enrage the client.

In any case, your interview is not the place to over sell your skills, education, job responsibilities nor your salary. Honesty is the key characteristic employers look for in candidates. If they can not trust you for 40 minutes, your probably not getting the job.

Remember, once you're hired, the client is expecting you to deliver. The bottom line is, occupational lies can follow you throughout your career.

One other example, I recall a candidate who interviewed with my firm for a Sr. Analyst position. In the interview, the candidate referenced working on a major project in Washington D.C. She shared that her direct supervisor was the Executive Vice President who managed a multimillion dollar division of that project. She left the project on excellent terms and mentioned that she had a great relationship with the EVP.

I was truly impressed with her resume, experience and communication skills, but noticed that the EVP was not listed as a professional contact. Unknown to the candidate, I worked on that project in a separate division and knew the executive she mentioned. I quickly made a phone call to see if my friend could vouch for the qualified candidate. What I found was eye opening. This particular candidate over exaggerated her role to justify the inflated salary listed on her application. The truth was, she worked on the contract, but was two reports below my dear friend (EVP). She's busted! I decided to pass on the candidate.

Always be honest! You never know who your interviewer has relationships with, and where they worked in the past.

The Elevator Speech or Your Brand Pitch

In the interviewing process the very first question will be something like, "Tell me about yourself". That's when you set the tone for the meeting. Nail your elevator speech! You have about 2-3 minutes to give a clear rundown on who you are. Don't act as if this is the first time you heard that question. Have your script memorized and ready to share. If you are not prepared for the first question, you will become the deer in the headlights.

Expect interruptions during your Brand Pitch or Elevator Speech. If your pitch is scripted correctly, it is the gateway to expansive dialog. Turn it in to an opportunity by engaging the script receiver in the conversation and lead them to hiring you. It's vital that you give a clear description of who you are and what you do best. Make it count, you may not get another crack at it.

Interview focus points

This is where your early research comes in handy. Once you find information on the organization, develop questions that are tailored toward your background. I call this "Counter Punching". Counter Punching is when you drive the focus of the conversation by steering the topics toward your objective. Candidates can find "Counter Punching" questions in the job description or Statement Of Work (SOW). Use these to script your intriguing responses during the interview.

Next you want to develop a list of skills & experiences that fit the profile needs. It is hard to bomb an interview when you've done your research. Learn to accept being disqualified for lack of skills. However, never be disqualified due to lack of preparation.

Likability

In my recruiting days, I would share information with candidates to help them get better at interviewing. Some advise would be technical in nature, but most was geared toward tactical likability. The basics like smile, be polite, have a sense of curiosity, and always be professional. Job seekers have to make the hiring manager feel good about the financial investment of the hire. Executives like people who are enthusiastic, full of energy and honest. There is nothing wrong with focusing on the personal connection with the hiring manager. Just don't get carried away with it. Be committed to showing why you are the best fit overall.

Professional Connection

Look for areas in which you can develop a connection. I was taught in sales to look for college degrees, sports memorabilia, technical interest, family photos and fraternity items. These are easy to spot in an executive office. They are also the most frequent topics amongst professional conversations. Candidates can try to find a common ground to break the ice.

For instance, one of my recruiters played college football at Notre Dame. In every meeting he would look for the Notre Dame Degree hanging in the client office. If he identified one, he'd immediately ask, "Did you attend Notre Dame"? That would lead in to a separate conversation on Notre Dame Football.

Sum it up

Clients expect a prepared candidate who can clearly communicate his or her value to the company. Stumbling during the interview shows low confidence and lack of preparation. This is not to be confused with being nervous.

I think most people get butterflies when required to speak to strangers. That is why making the right connection, staying focused on your task and being prepared is a formula for repeatable success.

Tips for interviews

• Script your employability brand speech. Who you are and what you do?
• Find your fit within the company. Listen carefully during your interview.
• Practice your smile. Present a pleasant personality. Clients look for someone they would like to hire.
• Refrain from badmouthing negative events in your past.
• Find compatibility with the job opening.
• Stay calm and confident when you don't have the answer.
• Ask "good" professional questions. Base them on your research.
• Refraining from using "Uhm...." when you are stuck on a question or statement. Pause, gather your thoughts and then answer.
• Be clear when communicating your expertise.
• Pronounce your words correctly when speaking.

Practice your interviews

Study your client, and anticipate interview questions. Go as far as, acting out a casual conversation with the gatekeeper. Several executives have admitted to practicing networking events to get better at working the room. If you practice something repetitively, your natural reaction will kick in during the live event.

Study your client, and anticipate your answers to interview questions. Go as far as, acting out a casual conversation with the gatekeeper.

Several executives have admitted to practicing networking events to get better at working the room. If you practice something repetitively, your natural reaction will kick in during the live event.

In the military, soldiers rely on "instincts" during live action. It becomes natural since a large majority of the time is spent on practice exercises. I guarantee that if you practice interviewing 2 times each day for 14 days, your interviewing skills will significantly increase. That's 24 interviews in two weeks. The return is a lifelong lesson on how to prepare as a professional.

Here is how it works:
1. You prepare to interview with a friend or family member just as you would with the client. (practice, walking in and chatting with the receptionist as well)
2. Dress the part. You don't have to be in suit and tie / skirt and blouse but get dressed with a purpose.
3. Have your interviewer prepare a list of questions managers may ask during an interview. (you can find tons of them online)
4. Allot 30-40 minutes for the interview.
5. Give your interviewer a summary of every job listed on your resume. Make sure you note certain milestones that are important in your industry.
6. Video tape or record your interview each time. That is twice per day.
7. Go back and review the tape with your interviewer. Share it with your mentor or professionals in the business for suggestions. (The tape will not lie to you. You can see how you are viewed by the client)
8. Look for personal mannerisms, posture, communication and other areas that may hinder you from getting employed.
9. Make improvements each time.
10. Continue this process for 14 days.

"Practice makes perfect!"

Chapter 14

Job search activity
"The Big Ugly"has a sister too

Job activity is the heart and soul of the employment search. It can be filled with good experiences on your way to long term employment. The keys to success is planning your job search strategy. Your job search strategy must have goals. These goals should be committed to identifying career opportunities that fit your career plan. Just as we established goals in your career plan, you must establish activity goals. Throughout this chapter, you will learn to be organized, develop job search activities, plan out your entire employment process and install accountable measures to ensure you stay focused. Your activity will dictate how soon you become employed!

Creating an execution plan for your job search begins with an inventory of the things you will need. Compare the list of things you need to the resources you have access to. Make sure you don't overlook little items like internet access. Let's not take anything for granted. You don't know how important the internet is, until you need it for job research. Here is a list of everything needed to create a successful employment activity plan.

Basic Activity Resources List:
* Internet (If you don't have it at home the library and coffee shops has free access)
* Reliable transportation
* Resumes

---

* Active and reliable contact information (phone and email)
* Interview attire
* Business Cards (Invest in your profession and pass out business cards)
* Social Networking Account (Preferably LinkedIn)

Telephone activity

Finding employment without calling one person is almost impossible in the information technology age. Most people would agree that you have to research the opportunities, and then make the phone calls to obtain more information.

For most job seekers, using the telephone to find employment is completely new and intimidating. Become an expert in communicating in person and over the phone. This means learning new techniques and getting over the fear of rejection.

The first thing we need to do is develop your phone objectives. These are goals that you want to achieve each time you pick up the telephone.

Your objectives are:

* Find out if the company is hiring.
* When are they hiring?
* Calendar of employment events
* What is the hiring process?
* Who does the hiring for the division?
* Can I apply in person?
* Does the decision maker use outside recruiters to hire?
* If so, what are the recruiting agencies?

Fact finding

Don't sound too eager or over aggressive in your initial approach. The gatekeeper will rush you off the phone and straight in the voicemail. You want to sound like a professional who is inquiring about the company and employment opportunities. Never lead the conversation with your employment status! Your status is not a priority to the prospect, so don't lend that information unless asked. Remember, you are just a professional looking for information about opportunities.

Concentrate on building data on each prospect. This information will become helpful when you meet influential contacts within the organization. Take the pressure off yourself. You will never get hired over the phone without speaking to a hiring manager. Just think of it as a casual business call.

How many calls should I make?

The number of phone calls will depend on how motivated you are to find employment. In the 90's, I wanted to establish the Washington D.C. market for my staffing and consulting firm. I took the Yellow Pages of the local phone book and began to "smile and dial". I averaged about 150 calls per day for the first 6 weeks. The first 3 weeks were nothing but numerous no's until week 4. This is when my luck began to change. I was hitting home runs, and my calendar was filling up. By week 6, I was closing deals and brokered 3 significant accounts.

It took 150 calls per day for 6 weeks to break a territory filled with competition. It is no different from finding new employment in an economy with national unemployment rates over 9%. Job seekers must establish a strategic dial count for the time allocated to make calls.

This dial count will need to fit within your resource capabilities, and it can not be a short term process. Phone activity is a critical task and will not stop until you reach your goal. How committed are you to finding the next job?

Basic Call Activity Formula example

Day of week	Mon	Tues	Wed	Thur	Fri
# of Cold Calls	100		100		
# of Follow up Calls		50		100	50

The formula above is a snapshot of a job seeker's dial activity for the week. Notice that the activity volume is staggered to allow time for follow up calls. Job seekers should build their personal call activity log with Monday. Mondays are the best day to set the tone for the week. Starting your calls on Tuesday or later in the work week will limit the momentum you gained over the phone. In this example, each day has a dial count and a purpose. Two days of the week are for aggressive cold calling, and the other three days are less intense follow up calls.

In your personalized formula, you may have to substitute a day for other activities. However, be organized and stick to the dial count plan.

The Cold Calls listed on the activity formula are the prospects you identified ahead of time that fit your Career Plan profile. Allot about 2-5 minutes for each Cold Call. That is an average of 5 hours of phone dials per day. This is a terrific start and the best way to get over your phone call fears!

Keep in mind, the 2-5 minutes of air time does not include having a quality conversation with a prospective employer. Those days you will have a limited amount of dials, but make sure the conversations are not wasteful. Every second counts, and hours can fly by talking to people who can't help you.

What to do with the other 3 or more hours during the day? Use that time to research companies, job boards and follow up with recruiting agents that are trying to place you. What ever you do, make the 8 hour day count. Don't waste it.

In the call formula example, Tuesday's and Thursdays were left open for physical activities such as networking events and walk-ins. Friday is a light day but commit to doing something. Try to schedule interviews or door to door fact finding on Friday when possible. Friday's are great face to face days. Everyone is in a pleasant mood and ready for the weekend.

Manage your call activity

The Call Activity Log sheet is just as important as the plan itself. This log or journal will help you identify who you called and most importantly, who is calling you back.

There is nothing worst than having someone return you call, and you don't know who they are. The Call Activity Log sheet can eliminate guessing and make the job seeker seem professional. The sample provided was created in Microsoft Excel so you can see how easy it is to develop your own.

You can customize your log to fit your organizational style. Make sure you keep the key points of reference: date, name, contact, company and notes.

Call Activity Log Sample

Date	Name	Title	Contact	email	Notes

Create your own luck tour

Create your own luck! Talking to the right person at the right time can seem like excellent timing. You will be surprised how your good timing can increase the odds of finding employment. Be persistent in your activities, and don't get discouraged with the infamous "NO". Have faith in the process. It takes time. Let the prospects know that you are optimistic in your employment search, and be confident in your abilities. The employers will sense your professionalism and patience during the phone calls. That will go a long way toward the first impression.

Walk In Activity

Walk-in activities should be limited to 2 or 3 days a week. Use the skills you learned in the door-to-door chapter to develop your walk-in script. Practice the walk-in tactic and outline your game plan. Schedule walk-ins around the your calendar of Cold Calls. A successful job seeker will have a calendar of organized activities, and walk-ins will be scheduled just like interviews.

What you need to know about walk-ins:
1. Get a map.
2. Locate every prospect from your Career Plan on the map.
3. Outline a commuting radius for your employment search. (Break your search in to 2 territories)
4. Find News, Press Releases and/or job board opportunities for the companies.
5. Develop and practice your walk-in script. Understand what you want out of the meeting.
6. Make sure your transportation is in place.
7. Schedule 10 walk-ins per week. Monday is Territory 1 and Wednesday Territory 2.
8. Start your fact finding mission.

See the example below to develop your schedule.

Day of week	Mon	Tues	Wed	Thur	Fri
# of Cold Calls	100	Walk Ins Territory 1	100	Walk Ins Territory 2	Interview
# of Follow up Calls		50		100	50

Tips: Building on the Call Activity Formula, you can include Walk In activity on the off days. See the example above, the walk in activity can fill in the Tuesday and Thursday portion of your calendar.

No excuses. Find a way to get it done!

What I've learned about job seekers is that you have a variety of philosophies to employment success. Some are firmly planted in the old school newspaper and unemployment office methods. The more technology savvy job seekers are more fond of a social networking approach. I firmly believe that employment activity is just a matter of personal and professional priorities. Job Seekers must have a balanced plan that includes traditional and untraditional activities.

Sometimes the job seeker will work outside their comfort zone. This is when most job seekers find excuses to take short cuts. In todays economy, excuses for failure can not be tolerated, if you expect positive results. There are too many unemployed qualified professionals seeking job opportunities. Borrowing a car, using a neighbors computer or making the local library your base camp, may be necessary for you to be competitive.

I tell inspiring entrepreneurs that success does not happen over night. I share stories that showcase the challenge entrepreneurs overcome each day to reach their goals. For instance, in my early years of being an entrepreneur, I used coffee shops to conduct business since I had no professional office. One of my favorite stories is how my partner would use the local hotel lobby's to conduct meetings with high profile clients. The point is, these are examples of how professionals work outside the comfort zone when necessary. I have not met a successful entrepreneur yet who will make an excuse for the lack of resources. In fact, every one of them have mentioned how that lack of resources during the challenging years made them better executives over time.

Do not allow the lack of resources or any excuse be the reason you are unemployed. There are companies right now looking for you to give them a call. Embrace the daily grind and anticipate accepting your new job.

I have compiled a list of job seeker activity excuses over the years. Can you find yourself within one of these?

Example:
A. "I am going to make a few calls after I take some time off."
B. "I'll look for a job after my round of golf tomorrow."
C. "I'm not a sales person so cold calling and door knocking isn't for me."

D. "I look on the internet every day. Can't seem to find any jobs locally."

E. "I have put in over 100 job applications. I'm just waiting on someone to call me back."

F. "I put my resume in over the website. It said to wait for someone to contact me."

G. "I have to get my resume straight first. Let me get that in order before I begin looking. "

H. "There are no jobs out there for my skills."

I. "The United States have shipped all of my jobs over to China or India. No body is going to call me back"

J. "The immigrants have taken all of my jobs, so why even look?"

K. "I don't have the internet."

L. "I was the Chief Executive Officer of a large company. I'll get a head hunter to find the job for me."

M. "My car broke down, so I don't have transportation. I've been catching rides for the last three months."

N. "I don't have a business card because my laptop is broken. I need to get that fixed first."

O. "I only have a few minutes on my cell phone. So I can't make 100 calls. I would have to go to my mothers house to do that."

P. "I can't go job hunting because of daycare. My sister can only help me a few days a week and you want me to job hunt everyday."

Q. "I take college courses at night. Making phone calls during the day won't work for me. I'll have to wait until I graduate to get started."

R. "I don't want my neighbors to know I am looking. We have to maintain a certain image in our community."

S. "I can't get on the internet at my coffee shop. There are too many people on the network."

T. "I had a job offer in Iowa but I can't go to the interview. My daughter is in a special honors program and I have to pick her up every Thursday by 5:00 p.m.."

U. "My transmission is bad. I will have to find a job from home."

V. "Networking events are for losers. I haven't attended one in 15 years."
W. "Its been a long time since I called around in the market. I've lost most of my contacts."
X. "I'm going to use a Recruiting Agency. I don't want to deal with hustle of looking."
Y. "I've got a solid social network with my fraternity and church. I don't need to make cold calls."
Z. "I'm currently on unemployment benefits and I want to milk that before I get started. I get a good check from Uncle Sam. He owes that to me."

Management and Measuring your Activity

I believe every job seeker must manage their reemployment process. You have to take a entrepreneurial approach and perform tasks outside the comfort zone. There are too many qualified candidates in the market to overlook the hard work that contributes toward being successful in a competitive market.

Measure your activity every 90 days. Log your good experiences, helpful information and critical leads. Use them to get better as a professional. Computer applications like calendars and notepads can be helpful applications to track phone calls and measure the success of your activities. Keep your journals in a 3 ring binder. Store the binder close to the phone so you can easily access the information when needed.

Activity to track:

* News and Press Release for each target organization.
* Leads for Hiring Managers.
* Dates given when the company plans to hire.
* Networking events that potential decision makers may attend.

---

* Gatekeepers you meet in walk-ins. (May need to reference them in the future)
* Keep every business card you get. (Easier to get business cards than to give a resume)
* Locations of target employers.
* Activity by territory.
* Resumes submitted.
* Interviews.

Activity to measure:
* How many calls you make each day.
* Walk-ins per week and walk-in success.
* Quality of your phone calls, walk-ins and interviews.
* How well your process is going.
* Measure your scripts. (Video tape your calls, scripts and practice sessions)
* Networking abilities. (At events and by chance meetings)

Your activity motivates others

Employment activities can be inspiring to others. Your success can be the motivation that someone else needs to get started.

Employment activity is where many Americans are failing in their job search. Strive to be the testimony at the next family gathering. Show that hard work pays off. Get in to a rhythm early and keep it going until you find a job. Don't stop! "Motion can create better emotions. Better emotions can change your outlook, and the right outlook will lead to success. Your individual success can inspire a national movement." All it takes is one person. Do you have what it takes to spark an employment movement?

She did it in less than 30 days

Here's a story of real employment activity.
I taught a workshop on employment activity in a small town in Tennessee. This particular group was full of professional women who were displaced or in transition. When we got to the activity portion of the program, I shared this formula with the class.

I expressed that the majority of students who have attended this seminar in the past found employment opportunities within 90 days. I also shared, students who attended the course and did not follow the formula experienced extended periods of unemployment.

The majority of the class was extremely quick to offer a professional reason for doubt, but there was one student in particular who said that she would put my formula to the test. This student would be considered a Baby Boomer in the workforce and had been in the service industry for many years. Because of her quick response, I was confident that she would be the one to see the power of her own productivity. I was highly confident in the formula. In fact, I guaranteed that any student who followed the full curriculum would have job offers in 90 days.

After reiterating the power of individual productivity, I gave my Baby Boomer the 100 cold call and 10 walk-in play book described above. My instructions were to focus on the first 6 weeks of activity, then evaluate the progress. I instructed her to record all of the successful activities and the ones that did not work so well.

The key words I stressed were; leads, fact finding activity, consistency, and continuous improvement (practice). She shook my hand and guaranteed that if the plan did not work, I would be the first to know. I knew for sure she would try to sabotage my program.

However, I also knew that if she performed half of the duties every day and executed her strategy, she would have job offers. She was determined and looking for employment. I had some experience with non-active job seekers in the past. Most of them give up before they even begin a habit. So, what would make her so different? Only time would tell.

The following month, I received a letter in the mail. It was my student thanking me for the training program and pushing her toward success. She said that the activity formula pushed her outside the normal comfort zone and in to a new network circle. She stated that making the phone calls were the most difficult to get used to, but once she found the rhythm, it became easier each day.

Her initial goal was not to prove me right, but to prove my system totally wrong. What she found, was hidden skills that she had not discovered before. She also found a better way to organize her job search and have a strategic plan while on the path to employment. I didn't find the job for her, nor did the job fall from the sky in to her lap. She created her own luck! The interesting thing about her response was that her industry knowledge increased during the process. She knew more about what was going on around her than ever before. That was critical in knowing who to target and who not to target. She didn't waste time chasing jobs that did not exist.

I share that story because this student, and all the other students who apply this formula, find themselves turning down offers over never getting them at all. This particular student increased her workforce acumen and became a source of insightful knowledge to everyone around her. She learned to ask good questions and how to research for leads. She developed the strategy, created her own career plan, identified her target market and implement the activity. She became a strategic opportunist!

As I would say in my classroom, "Commit to your activity and everything else will fall in to place."

Task Summary Page

This section of the book will serve as a tool to help you develop your employment search. Below you will find individual task from each chapter to cut out and include in your journal or portfolio. Use the internet and your creative juices to build your own forms if necessary. Good luck and happy hunting.

Unlock your potential for success

Task 1

Your Purpose question	Your "true" Purpose
1. Describe your purpose in life?	
2. What was you born to be?	
3. What would you do if asked to do it for the rest of your life?	
4. What do you enjoy learning about?	
5. What part of your current profession you enjoy the most?	
6. What do my peers say you're the best at?	
7. What did you want to be as a child?	
8. What is your favorite attribute?	

Task #2

Now lets dig a little deeper.
* Take 30 minutes and find a quite room. Write down all the things you like or love to do. (Professional and Personal)
* Close your eyes and meditate a while.
* Visualize your career path, life status and future goals.
* See if they match up with what you thought your purpose in life was.
* Also, compare them to your career path. If they don't match, then you are off track. If they do, then you are on your way to a great professional and personal journey once you put it all together.

Personal Purpose: (Write it down)

_____
_____
_____
_____
_____
_____
_____
_____

Professional Purpose: (Write it down)

_____
_____
_____
_____
_____
_____

Here are some tips for you to include in your daily, weekly and monthly tasks that can help you with being successful.

1. **Change your negative lifestyle to a positive one.**
   a. Separate yourself from negative people.
   b. Focus on positive meditation when you are alone.
   c. Speak positive things in to your life.
   d. Eat healthy
   e.
2. **Find something to Inspire you.**
   a. Take a moment of inspiration from your life and use it daily.
   b. Read a motivational book once a month for 6 months.
   c. Find pride in everything you do.
   d. Write down obtainable goals.

3. **Recruit a Mentor.**
   a. Find a person with a positive spirit to mentor you.
   b. Try to find someone at work to mentor you professionally.

4. **Do something physical each day.**
   a. Take a walk or a jog to jump start your mind.
   b. Try to work out if possible. It helps you mentally and keeps you looking fit physically.

5. **Read something positive or motivational**
   a. Read a religious passage, meditate or even pray.
   b. Find other spiritually refreshing books to read.
   c. Attend motivational speaking engagements.
   d. Buy motivational books on tape or CD.

This exercise is designed to identify challenges in your life (professional & personal) in which your attitude allowed you to overcome a challenge.

I want you to document 2 scenarios in which your attitude was the reason you failed.

Negative Scenario #1

_____

_____

_____

Negative Scenario #2

_____

_____

_____

Now document 2 scenarios in which your attitude was the reason you succeeded.

Scenario #3

_____

_____

_____

Scenario #4

_____

_____

_____

***This exercise can unlock your potential to become successful by answering some key questions regarding your personal attitude. Take these quick questions and apply them to your failure scenarios. Answer them honestly and look for the following:

a. Why didn't I do things differently?
b. Who really was the blame for my failures?
c. How much control did I have in the outcome?
d. Was it really worth going through the fuss?
e. How much would I give to do it all again?
f. Who did I hurt in the end?

Attitude can be a way of life, social perception, self concept and a learned behavior over a course of time. You can improve your attitude by learning new behaviors. Therefore, your attitude can influence the level of your professional success and personal satisfaction.

Are you employable tasks

Complete the Core Skills exercise

Exercise One: Using a separate sheet of paper or your book, develop a list of your **Core Skills**. Once you have done that, select 5 that best describe you. Use the list below to assist with developing your top 5 core skills. You may search the internet for additional cores skills to include on your list.

Caring	Appreciative	Patient
Advising	Flexible	Punctual
Reliable	Loyal	Mature
Optimistic	Active	Honest
Eager	Intuitive	Businesslike
Effective	Adept	Friendly
Innovative	Meticulous	Organized
Firm	Courageous	Dynamic
Insightful	Disciplined	Authentic

Top 5 Core Skills

1	
2	
3	
4	
5	

Complete the transferable skill exercise

Exercise Two: Using a separate sheet of paper or your book, develop a list of your **Transferable Skills.** Once you have done that, select 5 that best describe you. Use the list below to assist you with developing your top 5 transferable skills.

Computer literacy	Problem solving
Team Player	Ability to delegate
Supervise others	Audit records
Use my hands	Organize people
Repair things	Increase sales
Writer	Typing
Results driven	Meet deadlines
Print by hand	Handle complaint
Operate equipment	Plan agenda
Multitask	Research
Detailed	Budget
expertise	Collect Funds
Enjoy Math	

1	
2	
3	
4	
5	

Applied Skills

<u>Exercise Three:</u> Using a separate sheet of paper of your book, develop a list of your **Applied Skills**. Once you have done that, select 5 that best describe you. Use the list below to assist you with developing your top 5 Applied skills.

Certifications	Education level
OJT	Life Experience
Military Service	Politics
Authored books	Social service
Projects Intelligence exp.	Memberships
Training	Drafting
Forecasting	Bookkeeping

1	
2	
3	
4	
5	

Employability Questionnaire

1. Do I have the ability to communicate my skills professionally? Why or why not?

2. Can I elaborate on the skills listed on my resume?

3. Does my resume "best" describe my actual skills? Why not?

4. Does my education match the level of opportunities I am pursuing?
   a. If so, explain where your strong points.
   b. If not, explain your plan to correct it.

5. Did I actually do the things I list on my resume?
   a. If so, highlight your major accomplishments.
   b. If not, what areas should your remove?

6. Am I a "Jack of all trades and master of none"?
   a. If so, what can I delete from my resume to eliminate that stereotype?
   b. If not, what skills listed have no relevance in my career?

7. Does my work experience reflect my salary request?

8. Am I really a team player or do I work best alone?

9. Is leadership my best quality or am I better in a support role?
   a. List your leadership roles on your resume:
   b. List your best support roles on your resume:

10. Are my Core Skills my biggest assets? If so, which ones?

11. Which Transferable Skills will allow me to be "great" during my interview?

a. Are they currently on your resume?
b. Are they hidden within the fluff or in plain sight?
c. Which ones directly affect your employability?

12. Does my Applied Skills and work experience fit my current geographical market? (Your current City or Regional Employability)

13. Do I look professional in my business attire?
    a. How do I describe my business attire? (Youthful, Mature, Business, Church or Casual)
    b. Take down an inventory of the business attire have's and needs.

14. Do I need to work on my personal fitness and hygiene?
    a. What area do I need to focus on?
    b. What is my strategy for getting it done during my employment search?

15. Do I smoke Cigarettes?
    a. Has anyone ever asked me if I smoke in a interview?
    b. Do I smoke before interviews?

16. Describe your communication skills. Is it professional, casual or social?

17. Do I need to more education?
    a. What level of education will benefit me?
    b. Do I just need a refresher course?
    c. Does my target job require vocational training?

18. Am I choosing this career path because I love the daily employment activities or because I can make more money if hired?

19. Are you willing to work two jobs until you get on your feet?

20. Lastly, do I have the right Purpose, Passion, Attitude and Spirit for employment? Explain why you do or do not.

Here are some questions that will help you understand your current employability. These questions can also help you have a better understanding of your industry employability and target market.

Industry Employability Questionnaire

1. Where are the jobs for my background?
2. Did I review the local employment outlook report?
3. Who are the largest employers in my market?
4. What is the makeup of my current region?
   a. Manufacturing
   b. Banking
   c. Energy
   d. Telecommunications or Information Technology
   e. Defense/Government

5. If I am terminated today, are my skill set in demand in this market?
6. Am I prepared to move if needed to continue my career?
7. What obstacles are keeping me from making the right geographical move for my career.
   a. Family ties
   b. Money
   c. Transportation
   d. Fear
8. Am I actually living the right market?

Resource	Location	Information
Chamber of Commerce	Your local City/Town www.uschamber.com	Professional make up of your region. To include businesses, trades, industries and individual information for movers and shakers in your city.
Workforce Development Board	Your Local workforce entity: Employment Commission, Unemployment office,	Provide you with who is hiring, what industry and skills needed to fulfill the job needs.
Business Journals	Your local City/Region has a Business Journal.	Detailed information on industries, companies and economic outlook for your local region.
County Government Services Site	Your Local County Federal or State website.	Information on living in the area, doing business in the area and recreational/culture for the market.
Business Journal Book of List	Your Local Business Journal post a annual "Book of Lis". You can purchase for less than $50.00.	Scope of every major organization within your region. Outlines to employers, industries, executives, sports and healthcare information. It is one of the most utilized marketing media amongst business and sales professionals.

Build your career map

1. **Your beginning and end goals:** You have to begin with a goal. Some career plans have several goals that are in alignment with milestones. The key is knowing where you want to end while establishing where you begin. Start with the end in mind.
2. **Action Items:** These are marching steps in which you will accomplish your tasks. Each action item will be connected to your milestones. They can include task such as: internships, volunteer, job roles, experience, project types etc.
3. **Timeframe:** How long will it take to accomplish my goal? Some Career Goals will dictate the timeframe. Be patient. Keep in mind that the further out you set your milestones the more focus you must be to obtain them. Most people wash out of their plan because they didn't set obtainable goals.
4. **Education:** Your professional education is a direct reflection of your career advancement. Establishing an Educational Map that mirrors your Career Map is critical to realistic career goals.
5. **Milestones:** Your Career Map will have achievement milestones. These are action items that will keep you engaged and on track to your career success. They also are measurable in your evaluation process. They also reflect your hard work and determination to achieve your ultimate goal. The more milestones you reach the closer you are.

Career Mapping Sheet (Exercise)

Question #1: What is the professional job title/position I am striving for? (End Goal)

Question #2: Currently, how close am I to obtaining this position? (Beginning Timeframe)

Question #3: Will I need to change jobs soon to obtain my goal?

Question #4: What is the job requirements of the End Goal position?

Question #5: Am I currently in the right market to obtain my goal?

Question #6: What are the educational requirements?

Question #7: Do I have a mentor who can walk me through my Career & Educational Map?

Question #8: How much money will I need to have to achieve my goals? Will I need student loans, credit , etc.?

Question #9: What colleges, vocational schools or training organizations offer courses that I need to advance my career?

Question #10: Will I have to work during the day and attend classes at night? Will this add more time to my End Goal deadline?

Question #11: Can I obtain accredited certificates to accelerate my career plan?

Question #12: Does my plan include leadership, supervisory roles, project management or OJT based milestones? If so, what is my plan to obtain that experience?

Question #13: Am I prepared to change jobs, cities, regions or even move out of country to obtain my goals? If so, what is my strategic plan

Goal setting for the professional tasks

This Goal Sheet will assist you:

1. Establish clear attainable goals
2. Have a plan of execution
3. Measure and manage your goals daily Have a timeline that is realistic
4. Clear and rational Action Items (This is your plan of action. Very critical to any task but changes the daily outcomes)
5. Include some potential challenges you foresee. (Be prepared for unexpected challenges) Have a plan of attack for those challenges and
6. Assign a Goal Buddy or Accountability Partner to your goals.

Goal Setting Worksheet

APSI	Completion Date for Goal _____

Goal Definition Section

My goal is?
_____
_____
_____

Why is this goal important to me?
_____
_____

Timeline/When do I want to complete my goal? _____
_____

What do I want to achieve? _____

Measurement Section

1. Goals left outstanding: _____
_____

2. Am I meeting my expectations? _____
_____

3. Where can I do a better job? _____
_____

4. What I am doing wrong: _____

Action Steps		Target date	Completed
1			
2			
3			
4			
5			
6			
7			
8			
9			
10			
11			

Potential Challenges	**Potential Solutions**	
1	1	
2	2	
3	3	
Goal Buddy #1	**Goal Buddy #2**	
Contact #	Contact #	

Alliant Personnel Solutions Inc.
5100 Reagan Drive, Suite 17
Charlotte, NC 28206
www.apsicorp.com

Developing a winning sales script exercise

Opening Statement

YOU: Hi_____ (state prospects name)?

(Prospect: Yes.)

YOU: My name is _____. Do you have a quick minute? I am looking for some information on (Prospect Company Name)_____and I thought you may be able to assist me.

(Prospect: Sure. What you need?)

YOU: Great! (name)_____, I am a _____ who is certified in _____. I came across your contact information through (Referral, Social Media or Internet)_____. I am in the process of deciding on a career move to your organization and I had a few questions regarding (prospect company name or division) _____.

(Prospect: Are you looking for a job?)

YOU: Yes, I am always open to new opportunities but I have found success in speaking to decision makers within the prospect organization before seeking employment there. I want make sure my skills are a good fit first. Professionals like you who understand the needs of the company and I hoped that you could share some information with me..

YOU: With your permission, I was hoping to ask you a few questions to see if I would be a skill set fit at (Company Name)_____?

(Prospect: OK. I have a few minutes)

Sample questions YOU ask the prospect: (you must modify your questions based on the direction of the conversation)

1. What is your specific role at (Company Name) _____?
2. Does your business group hire professionals like me?
3. If not, what about other groups?
4. Does (Company Name)_____ hire (your skill sets here)_____?
5. Are you involved in the hiring process at all?
6. How often does your business group hire (your skill sets here) _____ or any similar skill sets?
7. Is there someone you can refer me to within the business group who manages the hiring process?
8. I understand (Company Name here)_____ was awarded a project recently does that project affect your business group?
9. Will (Company Name here)_____ need additional skills to fulfill the project obligations over the next 6 months?
10. Is there anyone I can speak to that can help me submit a resume for those future openings?
11. Does it make sense for someone with my background to pursue employment at (Company Name)_____?

The Close
YOU: Where do you suggest I go from here?

(Allow your prospect the ability to suggestion your next move)

The Double Close
YOU: I would like to thank you for your time today. I know your time is very important to you and I hope that I didn't waste it.

YOU: I would like to send you a thank you card. What is a good address to send it to?

(Prospect: No, you don't have to do that)

YOU: Well (Prospects Name)_____, in these economic times you don't often find professionals willing to assist other professionals in their employment research. You have given me some great feedback and I just want to thank you for your time.

(Prospect: Ok, you can send it to 123 EX Lane, Cunnigham, NC 28173. Address it to me.)

YOU: Thank you again. Can I share with (Referral Name given earlier)_____ that you and I spoke and you provided me with their name?

(Prospect: Sure, thats O.K.)

YOU: Thanks again. Have a great day!

Basic Business Wardrobe Inventory Check List

Business Suit
Color(s)_____ _____ _____   Amount:_____

Business shirt / Blouse
Color(s)_____ _____ _____   Amount:_____

Belt(s)
Color(s)_____ _____   Amount:_____

Handbag(s)
Color(s)_____ _____   Amount:_____

Shoes(s)
Color(s)_____ _____ _____   Amount:_____

Underclothing
Color(s)_____ _____ _____   Amount:_____

Socks
Color(s)_____ _____ _____   Amount:_____

NeckTie
Color(s): _____ _____ _____ _____   Amount: _____

Basic Activity Formula

Day of week	Mon	Tues	Wed	Thur	Fri
# of Cold Calls	100		100		
# of Follow up Calls		50		100	50

Calendar Sample

SUNDAY	MONDAY	TUESDAY	WEDNESDAY	THURSDAY	FRIDAY	SATURDAY

© Cegeon Calendars

Basic Activity Formula with Physical Activity

Day of week	Mon	Tues	Wed	Thur	Fri
# of Cold Calls	100	Walk Ins Territory 1	100	Walk Ins Territory 2	Interview
# of Follow up Calls		50		100	50

Call Activity Log

Date	Name	Title	Contact	email	Notes

Personal Development Plan

This section of the book is strictly for the professional reader who is serious about putting a plan in place. You'll find some basic steps to getting on track and employed. Feel free to use the outline below and begin building your Personal Development Plan.

My Personal Development Plan (Year)_____

Task	Due Date	Completion date	Signature of completion
Complete Compliance Wheel			
Complete Personal and Professional Assessments			
Find your core, applied and transferable skills			
Self and employability assessments			
Develop a career and training map			
Establish and write down your career goals			

Task	Due Date	Completion date	Signature of completion
Start social networking process (LinkedIn etc)			
Join 3 professional user groups in your career path			
Build your sales script and practice			
Begin your job activity with calls			
Start door to door fact finding schedule			
Interviews			
Job acceptance			

Evaluation Period	Did I meet my goal? Yes/No
30	
60	
90	

During your evaluation period, ask yourself some simple questions:

1. Did I perform the tasks to the best of my ability?
2. Did I quit on myself because of fear or failure?
3. Did I need any resources to assist my task?
4. What can I do better to help me accomplish my goals?

Index

A

academic goals, 45, 46
accountability, 62, 65, 66, 67, 166, .
Accountability Partner, 67, 68, 166
Action Items, 41, 54, 56, 61, 67, 164, 166
activities, 33, 56, 70, 76, 137, 140, 142, 144, 146, 147, 148, 161
Activity Formula, 139, 140, 143, 172, 173
Activity to measure, 146
Activity to track, 146
Americans, 17, 21, 147
Applied Skills, 29, 32, 159, 161
aptitudes, 2
attire, 32, 122, 124, 127, 137, 161
attitude, 6, 7, 8, 9, 17, 18, 19, 20, 25, 33, 39, 51, 52, 53, 54, 98, 155, 156,161
attractive, 22, 39

B

Baby Boomer, 148

beating the streets, 104, 107
Bing, 83, 84
Board Room, 87, 123
Boolean Search, 84, 86, 85, 97
brand personality, 14
Brand Pitch, 131
branding, 56

C

Call Activity Log, 139, 140, 174
Call reluctancy, 99, 100, 102
career development, 3, 8, 38, 53, 54, 55, 56, 84
Career Map, 41, 42, 43, 45, 46, 49, 47, 48, 49, 50, 164, 165
Career Mapping, ,40, 42, 43, 48, 165
careers, 1, 4, 30, 42, 56,
CEO, 23, 55, 56, 62, 94, 107, 126
Cold Calling, , 1, 93, 94, 95, 103, 139, 144
communication level, 95,96,
compensation, 2, 117
compliance wheel, 5, 6, 7, 8, 11, 25, 52, 54, 57, 171
compliant, 2, 6
Contentment, 19
Continued Education, 34, 44, 46
Core Skills, 26, 27, 157

D

Desired Outcomes, 88
diverse, 5, 113

E

earners, 52, 116
economy, 3, 21, 36, 58, 111,
    138, 144
Elevator Speech, 131
employability, 1, 14, 15, 16,
    26, 30, 31, 32, 33, 37,
    38, 55, 93, 102, 122,
    133, 160, 161, 162,
    171
Employer Reimbursement,
    46
energy, 9, 15, 16, 38, 54,
    132, 162
entrepreneurs, 5, 7,122,
    144,
evaluation, 10, 15, 31, 77,
    97, 121, 164, 172,
    173
Execution, 67, 136, 166

F

Facebook, 76, 79, 80, 98
Fact Finding, 106, 138, 140,
    142, 148, 172
Financial Initiatives, 42

G

Gatekeeper, 106, 107, 108,
    109, 110, 111, 114,
    119, 133, 138, 146
Geographical Infatuations,
    42
Goal Buddy, 68, 166
Goal setting, 60, 62, 63, 67,
    166
Goal Sheet, 63, 67, 70, 166
Goal Tracking, 65
Google, 26, 76, 79, 80, 83,
    84
Google+, 76, 79, 80
Grants, 21, 46, 145

H

Head Hunter, 112, 113, 145
Hidden jobs, 77 85,
    111,113, 117
homework, 74, 92, 94, 119
Human Resource
Generalist,   112. 113

I

Industry Assessment, 33
influence, 1, 2, 20, 75, 78,
    94, 102, 107, 156
interprets, 84
interview, 5, 7, 11, 15, 22,
    26, 32, 33, 45, 53, 89,
    93, 95, 96, 98, 99,
    105, 107, 114, 116,

118, 119, 121, 122,
123, 124, 125, 126,
127, 128, 129, 130,
131, 132, 133, 134,
137, 140, 142, 145,
147, 160, 161
Interview Focus Point, 131
Introduction Script, 89
Inventory, 32, 128, 130,
136, 161, 171

J

Job search activity, 136,
138, 139
journal, 22, 35, 140, 146,
151, 161

L

lifestyle, 7, 11, 23
Likability, 132
LinkedIn, 76, 77, 79, 85,
137,

M

Measuring your activity, 148
Men Interview guidelines,
125
Mentor, 24, 42, 48, 54, 62,
65, 67, 102, 104, 134,
154, 165
Milestones, 40, 41, 42, 45,
49, 57, 61, 134, 164,
165

motivational, 6, 23, 24, 122,
154,

N

Networking 71, 72, 73, 74,
75, 76, 77, 78, 80, 81,
87, 101, 121, 133,
139, 143, 146, 147

O

Occupational performance
measurements 40
operators, 84
Opportunist, 72, 73, 74,
105, 108, 161

P

pants, 127
passion, 1, 2, 3, 4, 6, 7, 8,
9, 11, 12, 14, 15, 17,
25, 33, 51, 52
passionate, 14, 15, 16, 52
peers, 2, 12, 57, 152
Personal Purpose, 10, 13,
153
philosophy, 51, 71
Playbook, 63, 64, 115
positioning, 56, 74, 82
Practice, 71, 81, 84, 86, 99,
104, 111, 122, 121,
133, 134, 135, 143
Preparation, 1, 131-133

Professional connection 132

Professional Job Seeker, 54, 54, 98

Professional Purpose, 10, 11, 13, 153

purpose, 1, 6, 7, 8, 9, 10, 11, 12, 13, 14, 15, 17, 33, 64, 98, 110, 134, 139, 152,

Q

qualified, 3, 42, 55, 98, 130, 131, 144, 146

R

recession, 3, 21

Retained Recruiters, 114

S

Sales Script, 87, 88, 89, 168

Scholarships, 46

Search Engine Optimization, 82

self assessment, 26, 30, 31, 40, 45

Setting Goals, 40

social change, 1

Social Media, 76, 77, 78, 79 80, 83, 89

spirit, 6, 7, 8, 9, 10, 20, 21, 22, 23, 25, 33, 52, 154, 161

Stakeholders, 78, 82, 85, 108

Strategic Target List, 75

T

Telephone activity, 137

temporary agency, 112, 114

Temporary Recruiters, 113

Territory, 138, 142, 143, 147, 173

The Big Ugly, 72, 93

Training Map, 49, 171

Transferable Skills, 26, 28, 32, 158, 160

transition, 2, 15, 17, 21, 38, 148

Twitter, 76, 80, 98

U

unemployed, 17, 20, 21, 46, 58, 76, 144

unemployment, 3, 30, 35, 44, 103, 115, 143, 146

United States Army, 65

W

Walk Ins, 106, 110, 142, 144

wardrobe, 124, 128,

wealth, 1, 97
Women Interview guidelines,
       127
workforce, 3, 11, 15, 35, 37,
       93, 104, 109, 111,
       115, 148, 150, 163,

Y

YouTube, 76, 80

About the Author

Scott is the founder and Chief Executive Officer of Alliant Personnel Solutions Inc. (APSI). Scott's vision and mission for helping others is driven by an attitude of excellence, ethical core values, communications and building good relationships. His strong determination to educate everyone he encounters has been the staple of his industry success.

Scott has over 20 years of experience in the consulting industry serving in top executive roles and board member for a national IT staffing firm. Scott has led organizations to significant growth in commercial and government environments. He has been recognized for building successful teams and developing new scaleable business practices. He was noted as a top earner for a staffing firm in Washington, D.C. before becoming a entrepreneur.

Before Scott set his goals toward corporate america, he served 10 years of military duty in the United States Army. Scott worked in several key roles involving Personnel Administration /Management, and supporting military operations such as Operation Desert Storm with the 3rd Infantry Division (3rd ID). During his military service, Scott became Instructor Certified and was highly recognized for his contribution to his country before honorably separating

Scott's professional portfolio includes serving in roles such as; Personnel Specialist, Supervisor, Human Resource Manager, Recruiter, Sr. Account Executive, Director of Business Development, Vice President of Sales, Vice President of Business Development and Managing Director. He sits on several community boards and works with mentoring groups to help young men and women become successful in life.

Scott has returned to North Carolina residing in Charlotte with his wife and three daughters.

Scott has a passion for education and works with academic institutions, corporate clients and non-profit organizations on building training programs. He finds time to speak to groups of job seekers and professionals on employment, training and workforce topics. Scott is developing new curriculum and collaborating with Wade Younger, a globally recognized author and organizational development expert on personnel components to the Value Wave Organizational Development methodology.

Visit Scott's personal website at www.scottacoulter.com

"In my speaking engagements I joke with the audience about being a recovering recruiter. In contrary to my sarcasm, I am so thankful for my recruiting experience because it allowed me the opportunity to develop a methodology that job seekers are finding successful throughout the US.

What I hoped to accomplish with this book was a process that would help every professional find their way in the workforce no matter what generation they are from. That is the number one reason I continue to develop new programs. I believe that if a guy from small town USA can find his purpose in life, so can you. I wish you all a healthy job search filled with employment and career advancement."

- ***Scott A. Coulter, CSS, Chairman CEO APSI***